SELL TO SURVIVE

Why
your life
depends on
selling!

TO: _____

FROM: _____

Published by Card1 Publications, Inc.

SELL TO SURVIVE

Why your life depends on selling!

GRANT CARDONE

Published by Card1 Publications, Inc.

Published by Card1 Publications, Inc.
1401 Oriole Drive
Los Angeles, CA 90069
800-368-5771
www.grantcardone.com

ISBN 978-1-60725-251-1

Printed in the United States of America

What Others are Saying...

"Grant Cardone's book 'Sell to Survive' is not just for salespeople. It's a book on effective persuasion for anyone – parents, teachers, managers, coaches, etc. – who needs to influence and motivate the behavior of others."
Dr. Tony Alessandra,
Author of "The Platinum Rule"

"Grant Cardone delivers a fresh, innovative approach to maximizing your personal potential and success. This book will show you how to apply proven techniques to achieve your goals personally and professionally. Brilliant, innovative and insightful."
Joseph W. Lineberry,
Microsoft Corporation

"This is a book that should be required reading for all high school and college students! It's jammed-packed with information for not only the professional sales person but for anyone that wants to get others supporting their efforts, dreams and goals."
Jessie Schwartzburg,
Author and Speaker Consultant

"In 'Sell to Survive,' Grant will show you how to start with nothing and become wealthy with his proven strategies. This is a must-read for anyone who has the desire to be successful in sales and in life."
Bryan Hardman,
GSM, Monument Chevrolet

This book is dedicated to my father, Curtis Cardone Sr., who truly loved people and who was greatly respected by both his family and his community. My father had great admiration for salespeople and the sales industry, and he was a firm believer that selling was a prerequisite to a person creating success in any area of life.

Why You Should Read This Book

Every person is constantly selling something, whether they know it or not! It might be a product, a service, or just simply a viewpoint. There isn't a person alive who doesn't need to know how to sell and influence others in order to improve his life. Most people have no idea how much their lives depend on this skill, and even fewer know the formulas and laws of selling. The first thing you will learn in this book is how absolutely vital this thing called selling is to your success, your family and your life. Secondly, you will learn very simple and basic principles that will make you an expert at getting others to agree with you and support you, assuring that you will accomplish what you want in any situation.

Take a close look at any successful person, and I guarantee you, they are experts at getting others "sold" on them as leaders and on their ideas. They successfully sold others to a point that people were willing to support this person, get behind him and make his ideas a reality. No success is ever achieved without being able to convince others to support you. The ability to get others to believe in you and to be "sold" on you is the only true secret to success, and is that critical point that ensures your dreams become reality and that you get what you want in your life!

In selling, like in all games, there are precise formulas and rules. Do you know the rules of persuasion? Do you know when you are violating the rules? Do you know when you are guaranteed an agreement? Do you know the exact thing you have to say to get someone to agree with you? Do you know the 10x Rule? Do you know the most important rule in communication and in selling? Do you know that every person has a power base they are not using? Do you know how to keep your attitude so positive that it will cause others to be sold on you? Do you know why people act strange around money? Do you know the Give-Give-Give rule that will make you a millionaire?

You need to know these things in order to accomplish what you want in life! The secrets to ensuring your success are outlined in this book as I share very simple, basic, life experiences, so that you, too, can reap the fantastic rewards you deserve. When you start applying the truths in this book, you will immediately start getting results and obtain a winning seat in life.

Be assured that in every exchange in life, one is either going to be the person doing the selling or the person being sold. Simply put: you are either getting your way or you are not! The degree that you are able to sell others, get others excited, get others supporting your ideas and dreams, is the degree that you will succeed in whatever it is you desire in life! This is called selling, and you cannot be successful, regardless of your career, without knowing this skill.

The principles of selling apply to all people in all aspects of life. Your ability to sell determines how fulfilling your life will be ultimately. This book will show you how to create the kind of life of which you've only dreamed.

Grant Cardone

Table of Contents

SELLING – A WAY OF LIFE

Selling is a Prerequisite for Life

Selling impacts every person on this planet. Your ability or inability to sell, persuade, negotiate and convince others will affect every area of your life and will determine how well you'll survive.

No matter your title or position in life, or what your role is in a company or on a team, you will at some point have to convince others. Your ability to do so will impact you in a way that will determine the very outcome of your life.

Selling is used everyday by every person on this planet. No one is excluded. Selling is not just a job or career, selling is essential to the survival and well-being of every living individual. Your ability to do well in life depends on your ability to sell others on those things in which you believe! You need to know how to negotiate and how to get another's agreement at some point in your life! The ability to get others to like you, work with you and want to please you determines how well you will survive. Selling is not just a job, selling is a way of life!

Selling-- (Merriam dictionary) the action of persuading or influencing another to a course of action or to the acceptance of something.

Who does this not impact?

When I say *selling*, I'm talking about anything having to do with convincing, persuading, negotiating, or just getting your way. This could include debating, getting along with others, exchanging goods or services, convincing a girl to go out with you, buying or selling a home, closing the bank to give you a loan, starting your own business, persuading others to support your ideas, or getting a customer to buy a product from you!

It is said that the number one reason a business or individual fails is because it is undercapitalized. The truth is, businesses fail first and foremost because their ideas weren't sold quickly enough and in quantities great enough, and therefore they ran out of money. NO business owner can build a business without understanding this critical element called selling! Think of any action in life, and I assure you that there's someone at one end or the other trying to persuade the outcome.

A golfer has a six foot putt. He putts the ball

and then does everything he can to persuade that ball to go into the hole. He talks to it, he pleads with it, he makes motions with his hands and he might even whisper a little prayer that the ball will drop. All the while, his opponent stands across from him doing the exact opposite. This example demonstrates that every one of us is always trying to influence a certain outcome.

The degree to which you can influence the outcome of events in your life is the determining factor of your success. For those who don't want to trust the outcome of their fate to pleading, wishing, praying and hoping, they must learn to persuade, convince and negotiate successfully.

No matter who you are or what you do, you're selling something. It doesn't matter whether or not you call yourself a salesperson because you're either selling something or someone is selling you. Either way, one of the parties is going to influence the outcome, and it will either be you getting your way or the other guy getting his way.

A sale is made in every exchange of ideas or communication, every time, and there's no exception. Deny it if you will, but that won't change the facts. You're a salesperson and you're one every single day of your life. From the moment you wake up to the moment you go to sleep, I assure you that you're trying to get your way! The fact that you don't have the title of "salesperson" or that you aren't being paid a commission is only a technical issue—you are still a salesperson and commissions come in many forms.

The Commission

Speaking of commissions: every time you get your way, you've just been paid a commission. The commission in this case was getting your way and you had to sell someone on that. Not all payments in life are monetary. Some of the greatest achievements I've had in my life had nothing to do with money. Recognition for a job well done is a commission. A raise or promotion at work is a commission. Gaining new friends is an incredible commission. Getting votes for a project you are pushing forward is a commission.

I find it comical when people tell me, "I could never be a salesperson because I could never work on commission." I'm like, "What do you mean, your entire life is a commission. There's no salary guaranteed in life. The whole world is on commission and the whole world is required to sell!"

It's been said that the best things in life are free, but I don't agree with that. The best things in life are those things that come as a result of a commission for some extra, well done effort! Happiness, security, safety, a great home, a great family, love, confidence, friends, your church, your community, and on and on, are all commissions for someone's hard work at selling others on a better way of life!

True love, the ultimate commission, is rewarded to those who find the right partner and take care of him or her and continue to create the relationship and keep it growing. There's no guarantee in life that you'll be loved. There's no guarantee that a relationship will get you love! First, you've got to persuade the person to take interest in you. Then you have to find out what they want and what makes them happy. Then you have to produce it and keep producing it. But somewhere along the line, you had to sell the other person on the idea that you're the one that they can trust to create a life with. If you succeed and exceed the person's expectations, you will get the commission of love.

Health is not guaranteed in life. Health is a commission for taking care of yourself and your mind. When a person successfully sells himself on eating right, working out and taking care of his attitude, he gets a commission of having good health.

The great benefit of children is a commission of sorts and is not guaranteed to every marriage. You still have to convince your partner to have sex with you, and even marriage doesn't guarantee you sex. If you can't close your partner on wanting to have sex with you, then you won't get the great commission of children. Once you have the kids, you have to continue to sell. Concepts such as discipline, work ethic, education, good manners, and homework all have to be sold. If you don't do the selling, they will sell you. Kids are the best salespeople on the planet. They're passionate, relentless and persistent closers able to break down their parents' resistance until they get what they want!

The point is, selling is about life and every area of life involves selling. The more consistently you can win at selling, the more commissions you'll get rewarded in your life!

So get it! Everyone on this planet is involved in sales. There are no exceptions to this law. You're involved in selling almost every minute of every day. If this is somehow distasteful to you then you have some misunderstandings about selling. When I say selling, do you think of a fast-talking swindler who can sell anything to anyone? Maybe you immediately get some image of a guy who's a confrontational, high-pressure type? Both of these images are negative extremes of selling and in no way incorporate the skills of a true salesperson. Confrontation and pressure are the attributes of the amateur who doesn't understand sales and resorts to unpleasant tactics.

When I'm discussing sales in this book, I'm referring to not only the professional, paid salesperson, but also I'm covering the everyday use of basic persuasion skills and how to use them to get your way in life.

Beware of False Data

The subject of selling, like any other subject, is full of false information that has been perpetuated over the years. This false data may be partly responsible for the bad impression of this profession and very needed life-skill. False data is information that is not factual but which is suggested about something or someone and is passed along. It is *agreed upon* and used as truth when it is not.

For instance, most of my life I wanted to own real estate and had a particular interest in buying apartment buildings. When I first got started, most of the people I talked to about apartments immediately told me that owning apartments was a nightmare and that I would have difficulties with tenants at midnight when the plumbing leaked. While tenants would obviously get upset if there was a plumbing leak, it is false data about owning apartments that actually causes people to lose interest in buying apartments. I've owned over 2500 apartments and trust me, the renter is not the problem with owning them. Not having renters is a problem, leaky faucets is just an issue to deal with. Of course there are problems with owning apartment buildings, but so what! I assure you that the problems are miniscule compared to the rewards. People who knew very little about buying apartments promoted this false data to me as an excuse for not buying them.

The whole subject of money is full of false data, most of which is passed on by people that give advice on money, but don't have any themselves!

When I was starting my first business almost everyone told me how difficult it was going to be, how much money it would take, how risky it was and how few businesses make it. None of these people had ever actually started a business themselves, but they had plenty of advice for me. You see, this is data that disregards all the successful stories of people like me who started their own business! I later started another company that required me to take on a partner. Multiple people suggested to me that most partnerships don't work out. Well, I can only tell you that while partnerships may be difficult, this business would have been impossible for me to operate without a partner. By the way, that particular partnership has lasted for almost fifteen years and we closed it on a handshake.

People tend to form opinions and give advice and pass on myths where they don't personally have any experience. Much of the data they pass along hasn't been fully inspected for truth even though it's been passed on as truth.

Take urban legends for example. A guy will swear to you that it was friend of a friend's sister that disappeared on prom night twenty years ago and how her ghost now hitchhikes along the lonely road between town and the old cemetery. You'll hear that same story in multiple cities across the country. If you ask him to give you specific names and dates, he won't be able to provide them, yet just moments ago he was passing on this falsehood as truth.

Many years ago, I was told not to move to California because "it was so expensive and the people were very strange." People who had never lived in California told this to me!

The same phenomenon occurs with sales and has given the whole profession and the skill itself a bad name. It's a shame because everyone needs the skill of selling to get along in life and the profession itself offers so much freedom and so many financial benefits. People continue to pass on the false information that selling is hard, that it's difficult to depend on commissions, that selling is sleazy, that you'll have to work long hours, it isn't a dependable profession, that you can't rely on the income and that it's not considered a "real" job! While this may be true for some, it's not the reality of those who know what they are doing!

Most of the images people have regarding a topic are very rarely based in reality. Certainly any negative images you might have had about salespeople are based on the past, which would suggest that they're not even relevant to the present because they're in the past. If I'm talking about selling, persuading and negotiating, you might get an image of a past experience or something you were told about salespeople and you're no longer involved in the present conversation. You're relying on some past decision, advice or opinion for your information. All images based on the past have very little value in the present and definitely no value in creating a future.

Selling – Critical to Survival

Regardless of your preconceived opinion, idea or evaluation you might have regarding sales and salespeople, you need to fully adopt the idea that you're going to have to sell no matter what your position or job is in life! Whether you're rich or poor, male or female, on salary or commission, you're always selling something or an idea to someone in order to advance. There is no exception to this rule and no way to escape this fact! That doesn't mean that you'll start wearing polyester slacks, white patent-leather shoes, while talking fast and pressuring people.

Take a moment to consider all the different roles you play in life. Let's say you came up with wife, partner, employee, mom, teacher, church-member, neighbor, friend, writer and PTA president. I want you to look at each of these roles and observe how selling is involved in each one of them. Maybe selling isn't your full-time career and maybe you don't get paid a monetary commission to sell products, but I assure you that you'll see how selling will impact your success in each role more than any other single ability you have.

The receptionist who wants a raise, the actress who wants the part, the guy who wants the girl, all rely on selling themselves whether they know it or not. A professional salesperson that depends on sales for his livelihood definitely needs to know how to do this thing called selling. When you're driving to work and want to get off the freeway, you will have to negotiate and sell the other drivers so you can access the off-ramp. When you find yourself buying a house and trying to convince the seller to sell at a lower price, you're selling. When you go to the bank to get a loan you will be selling the bank on why they should give you a loan. The actor goes to an audition and hopes to get the part. Well no matter how well prepared he is, he'd better be able to convince the director that not only can he act, but he is the right guy for the part! Start preparing now because there's no way to avoid the fact that you'll need this skill to do well in life.

The skill of sales is so critical to a person's survival I don't understand why it is not required study at school. The fact that it isn't taught in school, that it isn't required or even offered only further indicates the immense value of those that do learn this skill. It's my observation that the most important skills needed in life aren't taught in school. I spent seventeen years getting a formal education, and I can tell you that I have learned more from seminars, audio programs, books and talking with other successful business people at conferences than all my formal education. No successful business person would exclude basic selling, persuasion and negotiation skills from those things that helped him or her along the way!

A person's ability to persuade another is the only thing that will ultimately ensure a person's position in the marketplace. Academic records, grades and resumes will not guarantee you a promotion or advancement in life, but the ability to sell others will. All students should be required to learn basic persuasion skills, basic negotiating, and basic closing techniques, as these are fundamental to life! No other set of skills will better determine the likelihood of a person getting a job, much less being a success in life, than the ability to persuade, negotiate successfully and convince others to act!

As an employer, I don't always hire the smartest person or the most qualified person to fill a position. I'm much more likely to hire the person who convinces me they can do the job! I look at the person's ability to persuade before I look at his resume. Will I like being around this person? Is this person a winner? Does this person exude confidence and a positive attitude? Can this person convince others to take action? I'll hire the persuasive, positive and confident applicant hands down over the one who offers me little more than a fancy resume.

It's been said that almost 1/4 of the population on the planet is involved in selling, but these people are confining their thinking to an industry and a job type. It's incorrect to think of sales in this way. Selling is an absolute must for getting along in life. Breathing, eating, and exercising are not careers for most of us, they're requirements for living. So it is with selling! Most books written about sales are about the career of selling and exclude how vital it is to life

My wife constantly asks me, "How do you always get your way with people?"

The answer is simple-- because I want to-- I want to have a great life for us! Because I try to get my way? Oh yeah! Because I know how to sell, how to persuade, and how to close others on getting what I want! Whether she knows it or not, my wife is one of the best salespeople I've ever met. She's passionate, persistent and always seems to get her way--and not just with me.

This book is going to teach you how to get your way in life!

Chapter One Questions:

In the past week, what are three things that you accomplished which required you to use your sales skills?

1)

2)

3)

What does the author suggest is the number one reason a business fails?

Write down three commissions (other than money) you receive in life:

1)

2)

3)

What two skills will ensure a person's position in the marketplace?

1)

2)

SALESPEOPLE MAKE THE WORLD GO ROUND

Salespeople Drive Entire Economies

Career salespeople are vital to the dynamics of any economy. Without salespeople, every industry on the planet would stop cold tomorrow! Salespeople are to the economy what writers are to Hollywood. It's been said that *even God and the Devil need good salespeople!*

Selling is the last, great, truly free enterprise opportunity available today whereby an individual can work for himself, be accountable to himself and make his dreams come true. Literally with a pen to sign contracts and a commitment to excel, you can become whatever you want! For those who are willing to commit to selling as a career and who continue to learn how to master it, there are no limits. Do so and you'll be rewarded with all the treasures that exist. Learn the great art of selling and you will never be without work, as you're needed by others more than any other profession. Learn how to control the entire cycle of selling from start to finish, and you'll have the confidence to go where you want, do what you want, sell whatever product you want and know with complete conviction that you can have whatever you can dream.

The world stops turning without salespeople. If a product isn't sold and moved onto the public, factories stop, production stops, there's no need for distribution, no need for storage, shipping gets reduced and advertising stops. The burden of the entire economy of our culture today rests on the ability of salespeople! The economic engine of society relies completely on the ability to get products into the hands of consumers. If the consumers don't buy it, the factories won't make it!

Salespeople drive products, individual businesses, complete industries and whole economies. Like many people, I went into sales when I got out of college because I didn't know what I really wanted to do with my life. I decided to try selling until I found a "real" job. I went to sales because it was easy to get into and I didn't have to make any life changing decisions to do so. Even after making my decision, my family, friends and teachers rebuked me saying that I should get a "real job."

The problem for me was the so-called "real" jobs didn't appear to pay "real" money and they looked like boring traps that sap the life out of people. The only thing I could associate these "real" jobs with were the teachers who were promoting them. These "real" jobs come with "real" titles like doctor, lawyer, accountant, nurse, chemist, engineer, stock broker, chiropractor, etc. But the funny thing is, every one of these professionals had to sell themselves to others to make it in their careers! Their success in life is utterly dependant on one skill more than any other, and that skill is selling!

Sales or College?

It's a phenomenal mistake that the culture today doesn't value selling enough to teach courses on it! Not once throughout my entire formal education was selling introduced as an option. How respectable and desirable can the field be if it's not taught in school I wondered? There must be something wrong with this thing called sales if it's not offered in high school or college. If the subject isn't recognized or taught by the great "learning institutions" of the world it must not be a real career. Right? Wrong! No one taught me about money or investing or real estate in school. But that doesn't mean that those subjects aren't valuable. Schools don't teach people how to make a marriage successful or how to raise children, and what could be more valuable than that?

Many young people attending my seminars have told me that they were torn between going to college and continuing with their sales career. My response has always been the same. While the schools teach people very needed basics to get along in life and the work-world, no school can make a great person. You will learn absolutely necessary requirements in school, you might make some great connections, but schools are not capable of making a person successful. Only by application will you or anyone become successful or great in a field.

Survey the top one hundred most financially successful people in the world today, and I dare you to find one who attributes his success to his formal education. Many of them didn't even go the traditional route. That is not to suggest that schools are bad or are a waste of time by any means; but it is not "the thing" that causes people to do great things. Look around and you will find the school systems we have today producing a workforce of people who are able to remember what they read rather than apply what they learned. While you will learn many very needed basics, you won't learn how to balance a check book, how to increase your net worth, how to save money, how to negotiate a great deal, how to communicate, how to resolve problems or how to increase your value in the marketplace. You will only learn that after school or by seeking other information outside schools. That is what most people know they need to do in order to really improve their abilities. A basic education, while very necessary, cannot be considered an "end all." While there are some great teachers in the school system, it's unfortunate that due to the ridiculously low salaries, many of them are only regurgitating curriculums and forcing students to study courses and subjects that will never be used in their day-to-day lives. Ask any business owner what his greatest problem is, and it will always be the same. He can't find people that can think independently, that can solve problems, that can increase his business and help him expand his company.

Schools teach students English, math, grammar, chemistry, history, geography, which are absolutely necessary, but then never take the time to teach something as important as selling, persuading and really meeting an employer's needs. The schools, for whatever reason, are just not set up to teach the things that may make the biggest difference. I don't know why that is, but I can tell you that I know salespeople who are making more money than heart surgeons and with far less liability and much less stress!

All Professions Rely on Sales

I know for a fact that for a person to have a great life, they'll have to know and apply the skills of any great salesperson. You can hire a doctor, a lawyer or an architect, but you can't get along in life without the ability to communicate, persuade, negotiate and close.

These skills will prove more useful and vital than anything you'll learn through a formal education. I'm not suggesting that these other areas of knowledge are not valuable and worthy, because they are. I'm only demonstrating that selling is valuable and that it's a worthy and respectable profession and a vital life skill for all.

Rather than being an hourly worker bee, you can become a highly paid individual with no ceiling on your earning potential. While others may have decided that sales isn't a respectable career, I can tell you that I've been able to spend time with leaders in many professions from engineers and bankers to actors and film directors. Every one of those people has had to build a career around selling to get to the top of their industry. Of those top producers, every one of them has told me that they have studied books on negotiating, selling and persuading. Why? Because they understand that it's vital to their success.

Every person, no matter what his profession is, relies on selling. The politician wants to appeal to you and your interests so that you vote for him in the polling booth. The public speaker is hoping to convince the audience that his approach is the right way. The employee desiring a promotion will have to sell the boss on his value to the company. The coach has to sell his team on the idea of winning the game. The real estate agent must convince you to buy a house or to give him the listing. The mortgage broker wants you to refinance for the third time. The banker wants you to invest money in the bank's mutual funds. The waiter is selling the special of the day. The clothing salesperson wants you to buy the suit along with three shirts, two ties and wants you to apply for the department store's credit card.

Selling never ends and it includes everyone. Those who can sell, persuade and close are the ones who survive the best, regardless of the line of work.

I'll let you come to your own conclusions about why selling is neither respected as a profession nor taught in schools. Maybe it's because there have been a handful of criminal salespeople over the years who have ruined the reputation for all. These are not salespeople; they're crooks. But you'll find criminals and con men in every field including medicine, law, dentistry, teaching, politics and certainly psychiatry.

I'll tell you the fact of which I'm sure: no person will ever gain true power and stature in the world without the ability to persuade others. The ability to communicate and convince others is either an asset or a liability for you. No matter what your ambitions are, you are required to communicate to others and the better you can communicate, the more people will agree with you. The more you can get others to agree with you, the more you can have your way in life. The more you get your way in life, the more you will enjoy life.

Any questions? Call 800-368-5771

Chapter Two Questions:

What are three freedoms that come from selling?

1)

2)

3)

What are four things that depend upon sales people?

1)

2)

3)

4)

In your own words write the importance of sales to the economy:

What does the author suggest is either an asset or a liability when it comes to selling and how does this affect your life?

PROFESSIONAL OR AMATEUR?

The Professional

Step into my world and let me unveil the secrets of the professional seller and how you can become one! Even if selling isn't your career, you should be a professional in order to get more out of life! I tell attendees in my Money Seminar, "If you want to get rich, learn how to sell." I became a professional at selling when I was twenty-six-years old after years of research and intense study on the subject. The hard work was well worth it, and the rest of my life changed as a result of my learning this little understood life skill. Every business I have started, every dollar I have earned and all the great things that have happened in my life were a result of learning this ability.

Three-quarters of population earth have no clue that the successes they will experience in their life and career depend solely on selling. If they don't know how to sell, they will not be successful. While selling may not be your main occupation, hopefully by now you are convinced that selling is essential to your life. No dream can ever become a reality without successfully selling it to others.

Professional: *(of a person) engaged in a specified activity as one's main paid occupation rather than as a pastime.*

It is my experience that ninety-nine percent of all so-called "professional" salespeople have only a slight idea of what selling is much less how to actually determine and predict results. What I've said is not meant to offend you in any way, but to inform you. If it does somehow offend you, then keep reading because sometimes the truth is tough to hear and this book will put you in control of your profession, put you in control of your customer, help you increase your income and transform you into a true professional. The real pros for the most part do not even call themselves salespeople but rather call themselves litigators, negotiators, moderators, business owners, inventors, politicians, coaches, fundraisers, agents, actors, entrepreneurs, financial planners, and etc. Consider Benjamin Franklin, John F. Kennedy, Martin Luther King Jr., Bill Gates, Martha Stewart as just a handful of the real pros of selling.

The Amateur

Amateur - *One who engages in a pursuit, study, science or sport as a pastime rather than as a profession, or, one lacking an experience and competence in an art or science.*

I've met hundreds of thousands of salespeople over the last twenty five years, most of whom were amateurs and did not know the first thing about selling. Is selling just a pastime to you, no different than passing time watching television? Do you lack experience and competence in this field? Are you not clear about what you are doing while negotiating? Do you struggle to get your way in life? Do you think there is no way you could ever be a sales person? Do you have disdain for this thing called selling? Do you hate rejection and even the idea of selling another? If any of these describe how you feel about selling, then we have some work to do.

I can show you how to become a professional, but you have to get clear on two things: 1) Selling is critical to your survival regardless of your career. 2) You must decide to become a professional and give up any ideas that this is for others and not for you. You have to decide that you want to start getting your way in life. Quit thinking that it's up to fate or the Gods. It's up to you, and you will have to shift your thinking and get it that your very life and every dream you have ever had depends solely on your ability to sell. If you aren't getting your way, then quit making excuses and decide now to learn everything there is to know about the only secret to success—sales.

The Great Shortage

For thousands of years, salespeople have been amassing wealth and accumulating riches, and these same opportunities still exist today. It isn't real to most salespeople that they can amass fortunes, but this is due to the short-sighted view of the opportunities available for the great and dedicated salespeople.

While there may or may not be shortages of water and oil on this planet, I assure you there are vast shortages of highly committed, highly dedicated and great salespeople. This is good news for those who choose to become great, for the world waits with it's fortune. While there are hundreds of millions of people that call themselves salespeople, there are only a handful of "the greats." The difference between mediocrity and greatness lies in being committed to the profession, coupled with the desire to be great and the dedication to learn the trade. Despite the popular belief that there are limits in sales, I assure you that the only limits you'll face are those in your imagination.

The truth is you can get paid whatever you want to with no ceiling. You can decide what products you'll sell, who you'll sell them to and with whom you want to work. The truly great salespeople stand out above the rest and aren't even in the same profession as the masses. They think differently, act differently and work differently. To them the job is effortless because they understand how to reach their goals. They're paid immense fees compared to their peers. They make selling look easy and others are certain that what they do is because of some 'gift' they were born with. Nothing could be further from the truth. I've never met someone that reached stellar levels of success who got there because of luck or some sort of God-given talent. They're successful because they have mastered the trade.

When the economy crashes, the 'greats' may experience small dips in production, but they always survive and the amateurs lose their jobs. Great salespeople don't have ceilings on their earnings and they know that their income depends solely on their ability to get in front of customers, make themselves known, get agreements, close sales and reproduce those results over and over again.

Only a handful of people ever take the time to really learn this game and master it. When I was twenty-five, I made the commitment to KNOW everything there was to know about the game of selling. I was finished with pumping myself up every morning with enthusiasm and *hoping* for great results. Enthusiasm is great, but it's not a replacement for *knowing*.

The amateur goes out and plays golf every Saturday with his boys, but he can't play with a master who truly KNOWS the game of golf.

The person who knows what he's doing and every nuance of his career, doesn't have to get enthusiastic; he is enthusiastic. When you know something, you can predict outcomes. He who can predict outcomes has true confidence and freedom.

Chapter Three Questions:

What is the difference between a professional and an amateur (in your own words) and then check to see what you left out by referring to the book.

Write down three things you have been told there is a shortage of:

1)

2)

3)

Now write down three things that you have observed there is an ACTUAL shortage of?

1)

2)

3)

What are the three differences between mediocrity and greatness as quoted by the author (check off the ones you need to strengthen)?

1)

2)

3)

When the economy dips, what is the significant difference between what happens to "the greats" and to amateurs?

CHAPTER FOUR

THE GREATS

Commitment

So how do you become one of the greats in your field, one of the masters? The very first step and most important one is to commit all the way!

Commit -- *to devote oneself completely to something.*

This inescapable truth is required for anyone to be truly great at anything: you must devote yourself completely. If you are a career salesperson, you have to devote yourself, your energy and your resources to a career in selling. If you aren't a career salesperson, you better get it to your core that your success still depends on this skill, and then you better learn it. You have to convince yourself that this is the thing you have to learn in order to get your way in life and that this is where you are going to make your riches.

How does a person commit?

What I do is eliminate any and all options and devote myself to learning everything I can about the topic. I become a fanatic, 100% absorbed, all in, a Super Freak! I stop questioning and get in all the way. I discontinue looking at other options.

Committing is as simple as picking a place to park your car. Find a spot, pull in and get out of the car. You don't keep looking for another space in which to park. COMMIT AND BE DONE WITH IT. Committing is when you make a firm decision, you quit wondering, and then you follow your commitment through with actions.

Once you've fully committed to a partner in life, its good advice to quit looking for new partners. You take what you have and make everything you can out of it. Can you find someone prettier, smarter, and happier? Probably, but that's not committing. Committing means you are in all the way, you are done looking and you make the person you have committed to the prettiest, the smartest and the happiest. I would rather commit to the wrong thing all the way than commit to the right thing halfway.

Commit and be done with it!

Greener Pastures

The guy who thinks the grass is greener 'over there' is the same guy who never commits to taking care of the pasture he already has. He winds up mediocre and miserable. What was he even doing looking at another pasture in the first place? He already has one that needs to be mowed. Remember, while there may be greener pastures, they're green because someone committed. Weeds grow in every field, and if you don't commit to it all the way, you'll neglect it. When you neglect it you'll start to dislike it and then you'll start peering over the neighbor's fence thinking what he has is better. It's only better because he committed. So commit to your career, commit to learning something you can about selling, commit to your product, service, and employees. Commit to learning everything you can and watch how much green your career will produce for you.

Whenever I commit myself to any line of action, I get immediate results. When I'm not committed all the way, I find results are delayed or non-existent. If I'm committed 100% to the customer before me, I get results. But when I'm with one customer and thinking about another customer or wishing I had a better customer, I'm unable to make the best of what I have. Commit and commit all the way.

When I give seminars I often wear a small gold pin on the lapel of my jacket that says 100%. A salesperson asked me if I wore it for my customers to see. I explained that while customers do see it and they are intrigued by it, I don't wear it for them. I wear it for myself. I wear it to remind myself to commit all the way. I don't get dressed for my customers; I get dressed for myself so that I feel good, so that I'm dressed professionally. I wear that pin to remind myself that I'm 100% committed.

Commitment is a personal thing and is the indisputable requirement for getting results in life and separating yourself from the herds. At the age of twenty-five, I had been in and out of sales for five years or so and realized that I was still looking for another career. No commitment equals no results. I had not made a commitment to sales yet, and I was not proud of my position or the work I was doing. How could I be? I was only average at best. I was average because I was not committed. Because I was not committed I was not getting results. Because I was not getting results, I did not like my job—it was all a vicious cycle.

To the degree that you aren't proud of the job you're doing, you won't be successful; and to the degree that you are successful will determine how proud you are of your career. The career you are in is not the problem – your commitment is the problem!

I decided one day (after years of being mediocre), that sales was not the problem, I was. At that moment, I devoted myself to learning everything there was to know about sales. My goal was to stand head and shoulders above others in my field and to no longer be compared with them. I decided to become a professional and be different than the "typical," average, mediocre salesperson. That's the moment when everything changed for me, and it changed immediately and magically. Right away my energy changed, my dress changed, my actions and habits started changing, my language changed and my results changed. Immediately, my pastures became green and my potential exploded. It was almost spiritual! No it was spiritual. It was so dramatic --and that is the magic of commitment.

If you want to be successful at anything you have to commit. You've got to be in it 100% with no other fish to fry. A "burn the ship" kind of mentality is what it takes to get you to a place where you'll do things that will ensure results. Get into the game as though your life depended on it, because your life does depend on it. The life that you've been dreaming of depends on you getting in all the way now! This is how I approach anything when I really want results! This is how I approached the career of selling and the moment I did, my life changed.

I'll never forget the first time I experienced the magic and power of commitment. One summer I was working on an offshore crew boat servicing oil rigs. We were off the coast of Louisiana and we used to sit around waiting for the rigs to call on us. When we weren't actually working, we'd spend our time fishing off the side of the boat. On one particularly lucky day, we reeled in hundreds of red snappers. As we packed them in what little ice we had on board, I listened to the other crew members who were planning to take their share of the fish home to eat.

For some crazy reason, I offered to buy up everyone's fish with the idea that I'd go out and sell them. At the time I'd never sold anything and didn't know anything about fish sales. I didn't even know to whom I was going to sell them. All I knew was that my gut instinct was telling me someone would want to buy these beautiful, fresh red snappers.

With hundreds of snappers piled in the back of my truck, I realized that I needed to create a market, find some customers and figure out how to convince them to buy my fish. I had to think *fast* because the ice on the fish was melting, and I was going to lose my paycheck and my inventory if I didn't move the product right away. As I thought about where I might find customers, I remembered how the bible salesmen used to come knocking on the door of our home and how committed those guys were. It was getting late, and I decided that if the door-to-door approach was good enough for the bible salesmen, it was good enough for me. As the ice continued to melt, I blasted through neighborhood after neighborhood announcing that I had fresh fish.

Knocking on doors, I rapidly explained that these fish had been caught in the Gulf that very morning and they were the best money could buy. After I'd covered the houses in the area, I went to businesses where I found more prospects, sold the rest of the fish, and I did it all before the last of the ice was gone. I learned about the value of commitment that day. I had a fanatical, have-to-get-it-done and no-other-options level of commitment!

Commitment = Results = Happiness.

I made more money selling fish in a few hours than I had made doing hard labor for *two whole weeks* and it all came after I had made the commitment to sell those fish. I had put myself in a position where I did not have any choice but to sell them or lose them. It was a do or die situation. After that experience I was "hooked" on sales, but would not become a professional for seven more years.

The first thing you have to do is to commit yourself to selling as something that is vital to your life regardless of your career (but especially if you are in sales). Commit right now and watch what happens. Commitment is like magic and nothing great will happen until the commitment is there! Most people do not attack their projects with "I have-to-get-it-done-now" urgency and therefore do not get it done. Most people never commit like fanatics and therefore never become <u>fantastic</u>.

The Power of Prediction

The moment I transitioned from an amateur to a professional (following my decision to commit and become dedicated to my career), I began studying the whole area of selling. I started taking notes on every exchange I had with my customers. I even recorded these experiences on audio and video. I would later study the material like a football team reviews playbacks of games. I didn't know it then, but this was how I gained the ability to predict.

To predict is to know what's going to happen next. I stumbled across this skill and found myself gaining the ability to accurately predict the outcome of situations *before they would happen*. I started to know exactly what I had to do every day to create a certain amount of income. I was gaining the ability to predict exactly how many people I had to get in front of in order to sell a certain amount. I then discovered I was increasingly sure of what to say and how the prospect would react to what I said. I was able to predict objections and handle them *before they even surfaced*. It was as if things had gone into slow motion and I knew what every player on the field was doing and would do in the moments to come. The ability to predict is the first thing that happens when you become a professional, and I reached this level of ability, I knew I was on my way to great success.

Prediction is the great unknown and, very often unrecognized asset of the professional. I've never heard it spoken about, but I know it exists. If you've ever read about any of the great athletes, they talk about this same phenomenon whereby they are able to KNOW what's going to take place before it even happens. Wayne Gretsky and Michael Jordan have both been quoted as having the experience of being able to predict where the play would move to and how it would turn out.

Years ago, I was selling a product to multi-millionaires and discovered quickly that I had a very short time in which to make my presentation to them as time was of great concern to these people. In fact, time was more valuable to them than money. With one prospect, I knew exactly what his objection would be when I got him on the phone, "I'll give you sixty-seconds, son." Having predicted correctly, I handled him without having to think about what to say or do. Because I had studied prospects like him and had formulated and prepared solutions, I was able to be responsible for the exchange and get results. This prospect, who started out difficult, became one of the best clients I have ever had and later launched my career in sales training.

How does one gain the skill of prediction? You have to start looking at everything that's happening, observe it accurately without emotion or blame and make a note of it. The ability to predict comes from assuming responsibility for what's going on around you and believing you can control it. You have to pay complete attention to and record encounters and you'll start to see a finite set of patterns.

When I started recording my phone calls and making notes of every exchange I had with customers, I immediately tapped into my ability to perceive patterns and then started being able to predict. It was so easy and so fast. I carried around an "objections" notebook and wrote down every customer objection. Later I would study my notes and start to see that most of my customers were making similar comments. My awareness was raised and I was able to come up with solutions. It was amazing how fast I became aware of what was going on. One customer would tell me something and I'd write it down. The next customer said the same thing and I'd write that down. When I began observing and taking responsibility for what was happening to me, I was able to predict what the prospect would say. More importantly, I was prepared to handle him. I had control because I knew. To know is critical to success, as knowledge equals power in life. To KNOW means you end up with fewer "no's." Fewer "no's" means a better life!

My production almost doubled from the simple action of observing. My confidence soared as my knowledge increased, and so did my income. Prediction! I could see the future, not because I was a psychic, but because I'd observed the past accurately. I didn't realize it at the time, but I realize now that the ability to predict is one of the first benefits received from committing all the way! I had become responsible, aware, alert and solution-oriented and was able to predict! Until you become a dedicated student you cannot gain the skill of prediction. All masters (in any career) are able to predict accurately.

Once you get some sense of possible situations that can occur, start taking notes and record everything you can. Record yourself on video so you can watch yourself. I started looking at what I said, my facial expressions, my responses, my tone, my voice, my gestures, and wow, there was so much to learn. I became addicted to knowing all that I could! To predict is to know, and to know is to handle situations correctly. This will increase confidence and increase sales. To sell successfully is to enjoy your job, which means you will continue to expand with more sales. Winning begets winning.

The Only Reason You Won't Like Selling (As a Career or in Life)

Do you want to know the only true reason someone doesn't or wouldn't enjoy selling? There is only one real reason and it is not what you've been told. It's not because someone doesn't like rejection; who does? It's not because they're lazy. Everyone is lazy when they fail, and most people are trying to avoid failure. It's not because they don't like people. We all like people when we're successful with them.

The only reason a person does not like what he is doing is because he does not know what he's doing! He is not winning and he does not win because there is something that he does not know. The doctor who can not save lives will not like being a doctor. The teacher who can not get her students to learn will sooner or later become disenchanted with teaching. A salesman who can not close deals will not like selling. Therein lies the only reason you would not like being a salesperson. When you do not understand something, you are not in control, and when you are out of control, you are not going to like what you are doing!

I met a guy named Scott Morgan back in 1995 and we were considering a new business partnership. I was giving a presentation in Vancouver and suggested that he come up for the weekend to talk about our new arrangement and get in a little skiing. Scott had never skied before, so I suggested that he take a beginner class. He arrogantly puffed out his chest and decided that a beginner class was beneath him. The next morning the two of us were up at the top of Mount Whistler, one of the steepest mountains in North America. Scott looked down and then at me and we both knew that he was in big trouble. He knew nothing about the skiing, let alone how he was supposed to get down the mountain. While I admired his courage, I observed that he didn't understand the value of training. Scott spent the entire day getting down that mountain and to my knowledge, never put on a pair of skis again.

When he finally made it to the bottom, I suggested that we start a training company so that salespeople would never have to experience in their careers what he had to experience on that mountain. Scott and I have been business partners for many years now. He's one of the most persistent people I know and has made a full-time commitment to help others through training so they can successfully take their careers to the mountain tops.

To Qualify As Great!

All greats are able to predict the outcome of any given situation and great salespeople are able to determine and predict their own income. If you are unable to effectively and consistently increase your income as a salesperson, you are not a professional, and there is something that you do not know and are not able to predict. It seems like it would be fairly important to be able to predict what you have to do to raise your income! If you're not able to predict the objections and stalls your prospects will give you, you are not truly a professional and it will show up in lost sales.

Regardless of how long you have been doing this, if you're losing more than you're winning then you need to realize that you're an amateur and that it's time to kick up your commitment a notch and become someone that KNOWS what he is doing! You say, "Man you're being harsh on me! I'm just going through a cold spell right now." Wrong! You're making excuses and the reality is, your cold spell is due to your own lack of understanding of your profession. You've been sliding by on amateur skills and those skills are showing up in your results. Anyone can sell when everyone is buying the product, but when there's competition and the economy tightens, the amateurs start crying and the professionals continue to prosper. The major difference is the professional is committed and knows what he's doing and the amateur is not committed and does not know.

A boxer is considered a professional boxer if he's paid. But if he loses every match people won't continue to pay to see him fight and he'll return to amateur status. He'll be knocked down to his true rank. Most business people are being knocked down by the economy due to their ranking—their lack of commitment and not knowing how to sell.

In my opinion, a person does not have to be

paid to consider himself a professional. You are a professional when you can predict results and get them. If you know your game you don't have to rely on luck—instead you can get consistent success and can compete with others at the top. Pay just happens to be the reward given to those that reach the top.

There are many professional mothers who aren't paid for raising their children. On the other side of the coin, just because a woman is a mother doesn't mean she's a professional mother. There are mothers out there that you wouldn't hire to babysit your kids.

Just because you cook doesn't mean you're a Cordon Bleu chef, but you can be a professional even though you're not paid for it. My sister is a professional cook, not because she earns a living doing it, but because she KNOWS what she is doing, she KNOWS the kitchen, KNOWS her appliances, KNOWS her timing and KNOWS her recipes. It's not just the preparation of the meal and the fact that the food tastes good. Hell! I can duplicate her recipes, but the amount of mess I create compared to her, the time I take, the effort I use isn't even close. I'm an amateur cook, and she's a professional. She has the ability to predict all that goes into preparing a meal and I don't. This comes from committing to being aware and observing the scene completely.

Just like there are lots of cooks and mothers, there are also lots of so-called salespeople. But just because a person is engaged in the business of selling doesn't make them a professional.

If you're a professional golfer it means that you've qualified by playing in tournaments against others and have qualified based on your abilities to produce results. And just because you're a professional doesn't make you a Great!

To become one of the Greats, you have to practice, not just play. To become a great golfer you'd have to commit ever fiber of your being to the game and still know there's more to learn! Do you see the difference?

Most salespeople are amateurs, some of them are professionals and only a few are great. Ultimately, it comes down to the level of commitment and dedication one has. The Greats can predict and that comes from committing, observing and preparing solutions. To the degree you can predict, you can respond appropriately. Prediction is the great trait of the great salespeople.

The more you're able to predict with accuracy, the more you'll be prepared to handle situations. Like driving: if you know what the other drivers are going to do, you can avoid accidents. It's not just about driving your car. You've got to be able to predict what other drivers will do and using observation does this.

Can you remember a time when you knew nothing about your job but still got it done? It wasn't consistent, your income went up and down but you still made it happen. You made a sale but didn't really know why. You missed a sale and you were mystified for days. Can you remember a time when you used sheer persuasion, even begging or pleading and the buyer felt sorry for you and you made the sale? Leave that for the amateur and the underpaid professionals and start observing now so you can predict!

Observation is the only way you'll acquire a strategic understanding of the sales process and it's the only way to develop your prediction abilities and become one of the Greats.

Remember, no matter what your job or role is in life, you need the ability to predict. You're either getting your way in life or you're not. Even if you're not a salesperson, per se, start observing where you are not getting your way and start taking notes.

Those who understand selling will get their way in life and those who don't, won't! Are you ready to become a Great? Are you prepared to pay the price and do the work? If you are, I assure you that it will change your life dramatically, quickly and forever!

Chapter Four Questions:

Define "commitment" (per the definition the author used and look up each word):

Write down an example of something you didn't fully commit to and the result:

Write down an example of something you committed to completely and the result:

What is the skill of prediction? And how is it gained?

What is the only single reason a person would not enjoy selling?

THE MOST IMPORTANT SALE

Selling Yourself

Only to the degree you are sold can you sell. This is a vital and critically unavoidable fact that cannot be missed if you are to become great at what you do. This fact also happens to be one of the most important tools you'll ever have as a salesperson and can be used to monitor your career. The bottom line is, if you're not selling to some degree, *you're not sold*. If sales are slow, you're not sold. If you're not getting your way, you're not sold. If you've got some other excuse, you're not completely sold.

In order to become a great salesperson, you have to sell yourself on what you're selling. Make this the most important sale of your life and continue making that sale over and over to yourself. You have to sell yourself completely!

I know salespeople that know the game but are not completely and absolutely sold on their product, service or their company. Because of their lack of conviction, they are not consistent producers. You've got to be absolutely convinced that your product, your company, your services or your ideas are superior to all others. Many salespeople believe that their products are superior and while many products tend to offer similar benefits to yours, you have to be sold that your product, service or idea is somehow superior. You have to be 100% certain on the fact that what you're selling is better than all other options. The fraud can not get consistent results because he is not completely sold on his product

This one point is critical to greatness and you cannot negotiate with this fact in any way. You have to be utterly convinced and believe in what you're selling so strongly that you become unreasonable. That's right: unreasonable, even fanatical! You've got to be so convinced that you won't even consider any other logic suggesting otherwise. That is not to suggest arrogance about the product's superiority, but that you are completely sold on it. You must never allow the consideration to enter your mind that anyone else could even compete with you. That's not to say that others won't try, but you have to be so convinced and so sold that you won't consider or allow others to think about any other option.

Throughout most of my selling career I've sold more expensive products than my direct competitors. I have also gotten more money for similar products to my competitors because I believed so strongly that my service, level of care and my products were superior. Whether this was true to others or not was less important to me than my own conviction. While I've sold products that were priced higher than my competitor's, I've never asked a buyer to pay a price that I wasn't fully sold on myself, and that, I believe, is the only way to achieve higher prices.

I have been accused of asking astronomical prices for some of my products I've sold. They thought that I was asking a high amount in hopes that I'd get more than the product was worth—the idea of "if you do not ask for it you will not get it." But the truth is, I've never asked a high price just for the sake of starting high. I decide on a price because I'm convinced of its worth to the point that *I would pay that price to have it!*

Conviction is the Make Break Point

One time I put a house up for sale and the best realtor in town told me it was worth maybe $6 million. I told her to put it on the market at $8.9 million because the location was irreplaceable, and I believed it was worth that much. I was 100% convinced that the house was worth the price because I could have actually made sense paying that price myself. I sold the house two months later for almost asking price and everyone in the neighborhood loved me! The new owner went on to sell the same piece of property a year later for $10 million. It wasn't until I became convinced of the value that others later agreed with me.

The amount of conviction that you have regarding your product is more important than the conviction that others have about their facts and figures.

The word *conviction* is defined as a "firmly held belief." It comes from the word 'convince' which is derived from the Latin word 'convict' meaning to conquer.

Conviction is the ability to be so firmly sold on your beliefs that you demonstrate to your buyer with such complete and utter certainty that no other choices appear available.

A sale is made when your conviction and belief about something is stronger than another's, at which point they give up some of their conviction. That's the moment the sale becomes possible. I'm not even talking about a product or service at this point. I'm talking about the conviction of the individual himself. The real issue becomes who is more sold on what he believes to be true? Who is the most believable and the most convincing? It will always be the one that is most sold!

The highly trained ranger in the U.S. Army is so deeply sold on his mission and so sold on the cause that he's able to do things that would appear superhuman to others. He's convinced of the need to perform at this level and he does! Why? Because he's sold on his mission. He doesn't think, he operates. He doesn't have to think because he's already *decided*. He believes in it to his very core and because of this he's able to achieve the impossible.

Alexander Graham Bell was considered a lunatic when he talked of inventing a device in which the human voice could be transmitted long distances through wires. He was told that his invention called the telephone was impossible. But that's the interesting thing about the impossible. It's only impossible until someone makes it possible! Look at photography, flight, space travel, email, the Internet and on and on. All of these things were considered impossible once upon a time until someone became sold on it being possible.

Why is it that some people do things that others wouldn't dream of doing? It's because they are SOLD on the idea that it needs to be done for some reason. To the degree they are sold and become unreasonable in their quest, they will succeed.

While it's unfortunately promoted in our society to be reasonable and sensible, this will not serve you in sales or in life. If you really want something great to happen, you've got to be unreasonable even if it means convincing yourself beyond reason that what you have is better. We aren't talking about some trivial pastime here like riding bicycles! Anyone can learn to ride a bicycle. This is about becoming a great in your field and to do so you have to be completely and <u>un</u>reasonably sold on yourself, your product, your company and your ideas.

You might be wondering, "To get to this point of being unreasonable do I have to be crazy or insane to be successful?" The answer is no. You need to make a decision to be unreasonable. If a person acts insane, it doesn't mean he's insane. It means that he decided to act insane.

If you're unreasonable in your belief and sold to the degree that you see no other options available to the customer that would make sense, it doesn't mean that something is wrong with you, but that you're unreasonable in your convictions.

Being unreasonable means that you are sold on what you're selling, and it is your conviction alone that will sell others.

You must be completely "IN" in order to fully maximize the opportunities before you. Do not even attempt selling another until you, yourself, are completely sold. To the degree you aren't sold, you'll have difficulty selling to others. Anytime you find yourself having trouble getting your way, look no further than your own degree of conviction in what you're selling.

Perhaps you allowed your certainty to waiver or maybe something entered your head that made you doubt yourself or your product just enough to shake your certainty. Whatever it is, find it and throw it out like yesterday's garbage.

If you wouldn't buy the product or if you have any negative considerations about how it benefits others, to that degree you are guaranteed to fail. You must be sold. You must get rid of all negative considerations and believe that it's the right thing, the right product and that it will benefit the person you're selling it to. It's critical that you do everything possible to convince yourself that your product must be purchased and that it must be purchased from you at your pricing.

Why should someone go into debt to buy your product? Why should they choose your product instead of someone else's? Why should someone do it right now and not wait another second? Why should they buy your product for more money rather than a similar product for less? Why should someone do it with you rather than the guy down the street? Why should they choose your company over another? If you can't instantly answer these questions you'll struggle along because you're not convinced. If you were completely sold you would have immediate responses to each of these.

Become so thoroughly sold on your product that your conviction is irresistible to others. This is not meant to suggest that you lie to yourself, if that were even possible. I've personally met thousands of high-producing salespeople over the years and have never met a top producer who got to the top by lying and deceiving others. What I'm suggesting is that you take the time to sell yourself before you try to sell someone else on how your product is superior to others.

Overcoming the Ninety-Day Phenomenon

I've met many salespeople who tell me that they started selling a product and did well with it for ninety days, but suddenly found themselves unable to close a deal. What happened? Management will tell you that the person has gotten lazy or that he's gotten too smart for his own good. Okay, so he got lazy. But why? He wasn't exhibiting laziness for the first thirty days and he couldn't have gotten too smart for his own good because ninety days at any job won't make you smart by any means.

What I believe happens to cause this ninety day phenomenon is that the individual was either being told to do something that wasn't aligned with his own personal standards of ethics or he's now trying to sell something that he's no longer completely sold on. Maybe he doesn't believe in the product anymore. Maybe he has disagreements with the product, or management, or the services or something that he's promising. He's refraining from doing something that he was doing for the first ninety days. Something changed!

Maybe he got some information about how the product doesn't help people or how it doesn't do what he's been promising. Maybe he didn't close a deal and started wondering why and then made up the wrong reason for it and continues to use that incorrect reasoning. This happens a great deal whereby salespeople come up with wrong answers and then continue to use these wrong answers trying to solve future problems.

Whatever it was that happened, the ninety-day wonder is basically no longer sold. Actually he is sold, just on something else. In fact, he's become sold that it's a bad idea to sell this product and he starts not selling the product! Not selling is also a form of selling, just in reverse. Something has impacted him to the point where he's motivated not to sell rather than motivated to sell. Do you get it? Something went out in his thinking and he's no longer convinced.

When production drops, this is the first thing you should look for and rehabilitate. This individual must be revitalized and resold on the product, the company and the services. Go over all of the ways that the product is superior and how it will benefit others. Find out if there's some counter-intention, disagreement or false information about the product or service or company that's in conflict with the salesperson's beliefs. Once you've handled that, ask him how he felt about the product or service when he was doing well selling it and you'll find him motivated and closing deals again.

It's incredible how many salespeople tell me stories about the competitor that undersells them and practically gives products away or how the very product they sell can be bought on the internet for less. I recently read a book called *Secrets of Successful Selling* that talked about how competition had reached levels never before seen and that customer awareness had reached a point that required salespeople to operate at levels never before considered. The book was written in 1952, which just goes to show that there's always been competition and there always will be. The problem isn't product knowledge, competition and smarter customers; the real issue is whether or not you're fully sold on your product.

Become so sold, so convinced, so committed to your company, product and service that you believe it would be a terrible thing for the buyer to do business anywhere else with any other product.

Are you that sold on your product that you think it's detrimental and unethical *not* to convince someone to buy from you? Get to *that point* and watch your production freak out! When a customer doesn't buy your product do you actually feel bad for them and lose sleep feeling like you've screwed them over because they didn't buy it from you? If you were *really* sold you would feel like that. That is sold! The person that is sold completely won't let people not buy because it would be a violation of their own integrity! Reach that level of being sold and I assure you that people will buy from you.

You might ask yourself, "But what if I'm not convinced that I have the best product or the best service?" Then get convinced and do so right now! Do whatever it takes to believe that you're offering the greatest product and the greatest service. Find the plus points and sell yourself on them completely.

Let us take an unhappily married man who wishes he had a better relationship. Perhaps he hasn't been paying attention to his wife and he's lost some of his commitment and passion over the years. What happened? He basically isn't sold anymore. At one time he was completely sold on his wife, so sold that he suggested they spend the rest of their lives together. Somewhere along the line he stopped selling himself on the marriage.

If you want your marriage to work better, then convince yourself that you have the best spouse on the planet. How is your spouse the best? What sets him or her apart? What makes that person unique from any other human being on this planet? What are you sold on? She burns dinner, she looks terrible in the morning and she's got big ugly feet! Setting the negatives aside, look at what sold you on her in the first place. Sell yourself all over again. Find the plus points and ignore the imperfections. Get back to being sold and doing the things that you were doing earlier on and watch the change. You'll be amazed to see what happens. All of a sudden she isn't burning meals anymore, she looks great in the morning and she's gone out and gotten a pedicure and a nice pair of shoes.

Get Sold or Be Sold

Should you lie to yourself? Of course not; but you've got to get yourself sold no matter what! Rather than lying to yourself, a better alternative is to do what a champion does: champions decide to win the game with what they have to work with. They don't change teams! They make the most of the assets and strengths available to them. They play the cards they've got and they make the most of the pot! They don't lie to themselves, they convince themselves that the only solution is winning and they commit to one outcome only – success!

Focus on winning whatever game you're playing in life. Sell yourself on what you need to do today to make today great, to make your relationships great, to make your neighborhood great, to make your life great and to make the sale. Find every plus point and sell it.

David beat Goliath not because he had any real chance of being able to, but because he sold himself on the fact that he had to. Did he lie to himself? Absolutely not. He became convinced that his survival depended on taking down the giant. This is what you must do. Get sold and get committed to the fact that you're offering a superior product or a great service that can't be beat. You've got to make it so true to yourself that you can say it to others with such conviction that no one would even think of challenging you.

Put Your Money Where Your Mouth Is!

One time a real estate agent was trying to convince me that this particular investment was a great deal and a great opportunity for me. He kept going on and on about how fabulous an investment this property was. But I wasn't convinced because he didn't *say it* convincingly. He lacked the believability of someone who is completely and thoroughly sold on his product. Like any customer who isn't sold, I started questioning him. It wasn't the deal that I was unsure about, as much as the salesman who was pitching it. Something just didn't add up with the way he dressed, how he presented his pitch and the rushed, loud sales talk. He sounded like a "salesman," not someone who was completely and securely confident about his product.

Finally I asked, "Since you continue to tell me how great an investment this is, how many have you bought yourself?"

With a dumbfounded look on his face he quietly answered, "None."

You might be thinking that my question was unfair because maybe he couldn't afford the product. Look, if it's a sure thing, why not pool together all the money you, your kids, your parents and your friends have got and buy it? If it's a *sure thing,* you're not putting anyone at risk. If your product is a great deal then wouldn't it make sense that you'd be willing to buy it yourself?

By owning the product you're selling, you're demonstrating your certainty to others by your actions, and actions do speak louder than words. That's the difference between a "salesperson" and someone who's completely sold. It's unbelievable to me how many people sell products that they don't own themselves! Every product I've ever sold, I first bought myself and was proud to tell people that I owned it.

Obviously, you can't buy every single product that you sell, but you've got to be *willing* to buy it.

You have to be so sold that you use your product, consume your product and would sell the product to your loved ones. Otherwise you're just a mercenary selling whatever for the highest fee.

Ice to an Eskimo?

I consider myself to be a great salesperson, but that doesn't mean I could sell any product. To the degree that you're in disagreement with some product or idea, you won't be able to sell it.

For example, I couldn't sell ice to an Eskimo as the saying goes. Why? Because it would be unethical for me to sell ice to an Eskimo as I just don't see the need. I couldn't and wouldn't sell psychiatric drugs of any kind no matter how much money you paid me. I could never convince myself that drugging people could possibly solve a person's problem or make his life better. I can only sell that which I'm completely sold on.

A finance and insurance salesman at a car dealership was having difficulty selling his products and he came to me for advice on improving his sales. I began by asking him when he last bought a new car. He said that he'd recently purchased one and he went on to tell me how much he loved it. Because he was sold on that car enough to buy it himself, his conviction for the product shined through when he talked about it. He was speaking from the heart. I went on to ask him which of the finance and insurance products he'd purchased with his new car (credit life, accident, health insurance and warranty). With a chuckle, he admitted that he hadn't bought any of those products because he didn't want to spend the extra money on them. The truth was, he didn't buy them because he wasn't sold on the very products he was selling. Because he wasn't sold, he wasn't able to get others to buy the products from him. You might think, no, he was just saving money! Look, if you are completely sold, you won't concern yourself with the money. You'll buy the product! There is no exception to this rule ever!

If you're having a similar problem, it's an easy one to resolve and doesn't even require that you learn anything about selling. All you have to do is buy the products you sell and watch your sales go up. People are inclined to do what others have already done! People will follow you to your chiropractor, your doctor, hire your maid or go to the movie you recommended all because of what you did, not what you said. To the degree you're sold, you will take action and to the degree you take actions is the degree to which you will sell others!

I assure you that the finance guy I mentioned earlier would be more successful if he were able to demonstrate through *action* that he'd already made the same investments himself. He would have been able to look at his customers with full conviction and show them that he'd done what he was asking the customer to do; that he'd put his money where his mouth was because he was sold himself. By the way, he took my advice and his income increased by four times.

The Vital Point

The vital point of having salespeople who are sold is missed by 90% of all management. Go to an Apple store and ask the salespeople how much they like their products. Those people are so SOLD you'd think it's a religious movement. The Apple people aren't using PC's at home; they're sold on Apple and you feel it when they present their products.

I went to a very high-end steak restaurant and I asked the waitress which steak was her personal favorite. She told me that she was a vegetarian! Hello? Is anyone home in management? What is this person doing in a steakhouse?

I would never hire a salesperson if they weren't willing to buy and use the product themselves. I also wouldn't hire a sales person who wouldn't buy the product because he doesn't have the money. If he truly doesn't have the resources, let's get him a credit card or payment plan and sell him the product so he can tell others how he loved it so much that he went into debt over it!

Additionally, I wouldn't hire a salesperson that wouldn't spend money. If a person won't spend money or tends to be really cheap in how he spends his money, he'll always have trouble getting other people to their spend money! I assure you that the less hung up you are on money, the easier money will come to you. I know of salespeople who are so "tight" they still have their first commission. While they brag about this frugality, I am convinced they would have reached much higher income levels had they not been so tight regarding their own money because more people would have given them more money.

If you won't buy it yourself, then you're not sold yourself! If you can't pass the simple test of being *willing* to buy your own product, then you'll never be able to sell others in large numbers.

You have power when you're sitting at the closing table and can look the prospect dead in the eye and show him that you've already made the exact same purchase that you're asking him to make. Your personal conviction and believability will take your career to new heights when you're fully sold. Buy the product yourself and you'll become a miracle closer and will be able to handle objections that ordinary salespeople can't! Be SOLD on the products, services and the company you work for and watch your prospects turn into customers!

Chapter Five Questions:

What is the most important sale you have to make?

What are four things you have to be sold on in your life?

1)

2)

3)

4)

Define "unreasonable:"

What does the author suggest is the make/break point in selling? (define it)

Write down three lessons you were given in life that suggest you be reasonable?

1)

2)

3)

How convinced does the author suggest you become about what it is you are selling?

THE PRICE MYTH

It's Almost NEVER Price

If you were to survey all of the salespeople in the world, you'd find that most of them believe that the number one reason they lose a sale is because of price. This is absolutely not the case and, in fact, nothing could be further from the truth.

Price is not the buyer's biggest concern and is actually at the bottom of the list of reasons why people don't buy. Most sales are lost over unspoken objections, not the obvious and apparent objections like price, payments or budgets, but the ones that the buyer doesn't voice. Getting the sale isn't about money; it's ultimately about the buyer having confidence that the product is the right one.

If there is a price difference, the customer wants assurance that your product has advantages in excess of the cost difference.

The Price Experiment

Most salespeople believe that if the price was lower they could sell more. But the truth is, they wouldn't sell more because they haven't correctly named the problem and therefore can't get the correct solution. I once had a salesperson that said that if the price of my seminar tickets was lower he'd be able to sell twice as many. Even though I knew that what he was saying was bordering on idiotic, I practiced the first rule of selling: "Always agree with the customer" and told him that I often wondered the same thing and in fact, I said that I'd be willing to test his theory.

So we offered a Grant Cardone seminar in Detroit with tickets at one-tenth of the normal price. Detroit has always been one of our best attended seminar markets and the person that made the suggestion about the price cut was thinking that we'd have the biggest audience ever. There was only one stipulation to our deal to properly test out his little idea and that was that he could only sell the tickets by sending out a marketing piece offering the seminar, the date, the price, the web site address and a phone number to call. He was not allowed to do a full sales presentation. The reality is, if you take the price that low you won't be able to afford to do a presentation anyway.

That seminar had the lowest attendance of any I have given in twenty years. It didn't even cover the cost of my airfare and the salesperson's commissions didn't cover the cost of the mailers. I asked the audience why they thought so few people came and they said that they didn't think I'd actually be there in person, but that it would be a video feed of me. If the price gets too cheap, people won't see any value in the product. Additionally, if price alone were the reason people buy, then the company wouldn't really need salespeople and that would be a problem for twenty-five percent of the population.

It will always take a professional salesperson that takes the time to sell features and benefits to handle the buyer's price objections.

It's Love, not Price

After the experiment with the cheap tickets, I doubled the original ticket price and attendance at my future seminars increased by over 100%!

Price is almost never the issue for a buyer, even when they say it's the price. More often than not, it is love and confidence. Do I love this product, because if I do then I'll pay whatever it takes. Is the buyer 100% confident that this product will get them what they want? Will this service do the job? If the buyer is head over heals in love with the product and can't live without it, he'll buy it regardless of price, assuming he can find the money to pay for it. If the buyer has full confidence that the product will solve his problems and get him a real solution, he'll buy it at almost any price. People will give their right arm for love and they'll give their last dollar for a real solution.

If you've ever lost someone then you know what I'm talking about. In that moment when you found out you'd lost someone special, you'd sell everything you had and go into debt for multiple lifetimes, just to have that person back in your life. Why? Love, baby– love.

You have to get your buyer to want your product more than he wants his money! He's got to want the product or the solution more than he wants the numbers in his bank account. Discovering what he's trying to accomplish and demonstrating how your product solves his problem is the essence of how you close the deal. Certainly there's the issue of the product being out of someone's price range, but that's the point I'm trying to drive home. If they really love it and it will really solve their problem, they'll figure out a way to come up with the money if they are absolutely in love with the product or confident it will solve their problems.

You can't put a price tag on someone or something you really love. And if you've ever had a serious problem in life, money was no longer your concern. Getting rid of the problem was your concern. Give 'em love, solve a problem and you will get the money.

If the customer can afford the product or service but isn't buying and is harping about the money, I always realize that he has other concerns that must be handled. If he were completely sold, price would not be the issue.

While your prospect may be objecting to price, here is a partial list of what he or she is considering: *Is this the right product? Is there a better product than this? Is this the right proposal? Will this truly solve our problems? Will my people use it? What will others think of me buying this? Is this something I am going to really use and enjoy? Will this company really take care of me and service us? Am I better off buying something else? Will something better come out next week? Do I know enough? Do we have all the information? Should we get an "X" instead? Should I join the country club? Am I better off with the money in the bank than investing it? Is this going to be a mistake like past decisions?*

If these considerations are handled to the buyer's satisfaction, price will no longer be the issue. The product or service that you're selling will obviously create different concerns for the decision maker, but trust me, regardless of what it is you have, it almost never comes down to just price. To the degree that you understand this you will be successful.

Let's say a guy is buying a birthday present for the love of his life. He finds something he thinks his girl will love, but tells the salesperson that is costs more than he would like to spend. What he's actually saying is that he isn't completely sold on the product being the perfect gift for her. He either doesn't love it himself or he's not sure that it's something she will love. This product is not yet making him feel good enough or certain enough to pull the trigger and buy the gift. In this case, I would acknowledge him, tell him I understand that it is more than he wants to spend but ask him for the right to actually show him something a bit more expensive just for fun. He said it was too much, he didn't say he didn't like it and he didn't say he couldn't do it! Also consider when he said it was too much, he could mean that it was too much for that product, rather than, *I can't do it*. Maybe, just maybe, he'd rather spend extra money and get a gift he loves more.

Move Up, Don't Move Down

Most salespeople make the mistake of offering something for a lower price when faced with price objections. This is an incorrect solution based on the false belief that price is the reason people don't buy things.

When you move the customer down in price or offer him something cheaper, he's less likely to want this next product if he didn't want the first one. This will then cause the buyer to think that you have no solution and that he's just wasting his time. By moving him up rather than down in inventory you'll get him thinking in terms of value and find out whether his objection is valid or not.

If he believes that his girl will love the gift and he really wants to make her happy, then showing him something more expensive will actually get you closer to a sale. Remember, he wants to make good decisions. At this point he'll either demonstrate that the first product was the wrong choice by the simple fact that he's now looking at the more expensive option, or he'll tell you that he needs to move in the other direction with something that costs less. Either way, *you've got him shopping with you, not negotiating with you.* I could even show him a completely different line or product knowing that we can always move back to the original. I want to exhaust my inventory, not my price!

I remember a customer once who told me that my product was too much money and I was unable to close him. He left me and bought a product for $150,000 more from my competitor. When he told me it was too much money, he was really saying, it's too much for the solution you're offering. You will discover that as many price objections will be solved with more expensive solutions as are solved with lower prices.

When I can't close a sale, I'll always try to move the buyer up to a bigger or more expensive product as the first solution to price objection. Although this may not make immediate sense to you, I assure you that it will prove successful. If they'll at least consider it, I know I'm on a product that they're still in question about. This is called "closing with inventory." I've had thousands of customers tell me either that it's too much money, over the budget or they get that uncomfortable money look on their face during the close. I'll immediately move that buyer up to a more expensive product. Why? Because they're telling me that it's too much money for that product or service or that they're not sure it will resolve their problem. The buyer would rather pay more and make the right decision than pay less and make a mistake!

Every consumer has made mistakes before and this is the number one reason why they hesitate on making decisions. It is the fear of repeating a mistake; it is not the fear of spending the money. It's the angst of making the wrong choice or buying the wrong product or making a decision that doesn't create the solution they were looking for more than it is price.

Always show your buyers how they can spend more as a solution to price and this will determine whether or not you're dealing with a real price objection. The worst outcome is that the more expensive product will make the one they're looking at appear more accessible and this will actually build value and substantiate the price. Never buy into the talk of the mediocre salespeople around you who believe that price is the most important issue or who promote the idea that if the price was lower they could sell more! Just look at their results and then disregard their advice.

One time a charity asked me if I'd help out with some fundraising. They told me about this one prospect that had the wherewithal to make a sizeable donation and was supportive of the charity, but they were having trouble getting him to make a financial contribution. They'd been working on him for a year and hadn't gotten a penny. I asked them how much they'd been trying to get him to donate and discovered that they'd been asking for $10,000. I suggested that they might have been asking him for too little. Maybe this prospect didn't like making small contributions and that it might be easier to get a larger one.

One woman looked at me with disbelief and said that this man was one of the cheapest people she'd ever tried to get a contribution from. So I took the prospect aside and in ten minutes had him closed to contribute ten times what they'd been trying to get for a year. He wasn't cheap by any means except in the mind of the fundraiser. In fact, he was one of the most generous people I'd ever met. The prospect told me that he hadn't contributed anything to the charity in the past because he didn't feel that $10,000 would really make a difference. All I did was ask him for the right amount that *he believed* would make a difference! The higher contribution actually solved his problem.

Tip: Your prospect is never the problem – NEVER! Salespeople are the ultimate barriers to every sale, not the prospect.

Salespeople Stop Sales, Not Customers

You have to get this into your head - *price is not your problem, you are!* Customers do not stop sales. It is salespeople that stop a sale from happening. You are the barrier to the closed deal, not the customer.

Give the prospect a product that he loves or a service that solves his problems and you'll get the close once he's got full confidence in the product or service and you.

There will be times when you'll have to handle the buyer on money. Sometimes I remind a person, "while I agree it's a lot of money for a gift, there's no shortage of money on this planet. But there is a shortage of people who've found the love of their life and who know how to show their appreciation for that person. Be grateful you've got someone to love. Now, how would you like to handle this?" Now that's selling!

If the buyer is totally convinced it's right, they will chew off their own foot to have it! If the buyer who's saying it's too much money found out that he had a disease and was going to die, but that this product would save his life what would he do? He'd find the money, buy the product and save his life. Why? Because he's completely sold on the need! If the need is important enough and he has confidence in the cure, if the love is great enough, price will not be an issue.

When buying a house for instance, the unspoken objections the realtor won't hear will be, "Is this the right house? Is this the place that's going to fulfill our needs? Will we be happy here? Is this going to be a good investment? Do I really love this place? Can we do better? If we're going to spend this much money, why don't we spend a little more and get our dream house?" The last one regarding lets spend more money happens to about fifty-percent of all buyers who are concerned with price. Those same buyers who use price as an objection will often go out and spend even more money, not less! Remember many times when a buyer says, "its too much money", what they're saying is, "it's too much for this product"!

I told you a story about a house I sold for fifty-percent more than the realtor said it could possibly bring. When the buyer came to the house, I knew she loved it the moment she walked in. Later she insisted on having an appraisal done because her manager said she was paying too much. I explained to the buyer that while I understood she wanted an appraisal, it would be a waste of money because the house wouldn't appraise for the price she was paying. I told her that the house was overpriced and because of that it wouldn't appraise. I went on to tell her that I'd paid too much for the house when I bought it, that the people before me paid too much when they bought it and that the next people after her were going to pay too much for it. Because of the location it had always sold for more than it appraised for and that everyone would always overpay for it, and it would never appraise. The buyer decided not to have it appraised and bought the house. She lived there about a year and a half and sold it to the next people for too much money. It's never about price; it is about love or confidence that the product will solve problems.

$4 Coffee and $2 Water

To be an effective salesperson you have to believe in human beings. You need to have a positive outlook about people. You have to believe that people are good and that they want to make the right decision. Your buyers are just like you; they spend money they don't have, they go over budget, they work hard for their money, they've made good decisions and they've made bad decisions. Like you, they want to avoid bad decisions and make good ones. People want to feel good about themselves and their decisions.

If you're selling a service to a business owner he wants to know that he did the right thing for his business and that what he paid for is going to make a difference for his company. If you're selling a product, consumers want to have certainty that they'll be happy with it and that when they use it they're going to feel good, look good and be admired by others because of the choice they made.

If people don't buy from you, I assure you it's almost never about the money or the budget, but about something you didn't uncover. If it were all about price, please explain to me why people stand in line for a four-dollar cup of coffee when they can make an entire pot at home for almost nothing. Explain why people spend two-dollars on a bottle of water when they could have gotten it from the tap for free. Explain why someone spends thousands of dollars on season tickets to the ball game when they could watch it on television. Explain why someone would go out and buy a sports car when they could take the subway to work and arrive there in half the time. Explain why you bring your kid to a professional when he cuts himself rather than stitching him up yourself! Love, baby love!

Consider how many times you paid more than you could afford and you *loved it!* Consider how many times in your life you went over budget because you found something that you weren't even looking for and decided to buy it on impulse.

Remember, it's almost never price.

Chapter Six Questions:

What does the author suggest is the main reason people don't buy something?

Give two examples when you told someone that you couldn't do something and used price as the reason when there was another objection that you never voiced:

1)

2)

What are the two main reasons people will buy something:

1)

2)

Write down three things people buy everyday that they love but don't need?

1)

2)

3)

Write down three examples of times when you bought something you could not afford because it solved a problem or you loved it so much you had to buy it:

1)

2)

3)

What does the author suggest as the best way to justify a price when there is an objection:

CHAPTER SEVEN

YOUR BUYER'S MONEY

There is No Shortage of Moncy

Before you ask customers for their money, there's something that you need to get straight about the subject. Millions of people on this planet have the false idea that there's some sort of money shortage. But the truth of the matter is, there's more than enough money to go around, in fact, there's surpluses of it.

Did you know that there's enough money circulating on this planet for every human being to have a net worth of one-billion dollars? One billion dollars! Are you getting your share? If you're not it's because you're thinking in terms of hard work and limits, not abundance.

Look out at the Pacific Ocean and observe the infinite energy created there. The Pacific never stops. Go out there and get as many buckets of water as you want. How many buckets can you take? If you took as many bucketfuls as you wanted, would there still be plenty of ocean? Absolutely.

Look at how much money is in the marketplace. How many people own homes, own cars, pay telephone bills every month and buy clothes and food. There are endless amounts of money and if we ever get close to running out they'll just print more, thus inflation!

Get over the idea that there's a scarcity of money because there isn't! There's plenty of money to go around. If you start looking for prosperity and abundance, you'll see that it exists all around you.

ALERT! If others have a difficult time getting money from you, you'll never find it easy to get money from others. Many of the best highest paid salespeople I've known are the most generous people I've ever met. They're less significant about money, not because they have it, but because they understand that money is to be used, not possessed. Because they know this, they don't have trouble getting others to part with it.

Your Buyer and His Money

Your buyer becomes quite funny when it comes to decision time and giving you the money. It's as if money somehow identifies them or they feel they'll be different once they give it to someone else. When it comes to actually parting with the money, they can act strange and start making excuses, they generate odd stories and may even alter the truth a bit. The trained professional knows how to stay in the deal, knows how to handle objections and stalls, knows how to persist and can do so without appearing to pressure the customer.

It's even funnier when you consider that most people aren't giving you money, they're merely transferring numbers from one bank account to another. In most cases they aren't even paying for it, someone else is. But they say, "I can't afford this." Of course you can not afford it, that is why we have banks!

I've had people tell me that my price is too high and it wasn't even their money. When the actual money guy got involved, he immediately said 'yes' and never once mentioned the price.

Some of the most difficult buyers I've ever been involved with later thanked me profusely for hanging in there with them, working through the price issues and helping them make the right decision. Love your product, love your service, love your customer and love yourself enough to learn how to "hard sell." If you need some help handling these price objections, then get my complete audio program on closing the deal. It will change your life.

Second Money Is Easier Than First Money

I discovered the second money phenomenon by accident one week when I was on fire selling everybody that I called on. It was one of those freak moments when everything was easy and effortless. Every prospect I was working with was buying from me and it seemed as though I'd walked through some magical closing portal in the universe. I'd spent hours selling this executive who was trying to make sense of the product being affordable for his company. He finally submitted to my logic and persuasion and agreed to make the purchase.

Upon delivery of that product I decided to see if I could move them up another level, as I truly believed that it would be a better investment for the company. I knew that they'd already gone over budget, but I had to try anyway. I suggested to them that since they were already paying more than they were comfortable with, why not go all the way and move up another level. They looked at each other and turned to me in astonishment, "Actually," one of the guys said, "We were going to ask you to do just that. We're already paying more than we can afford-- we'll just have to produce a little more to make it work." In that moment I'd stumbled across one of the great secrets of selling. *Second money is easier to get than the first money.*

Startled by this discovery, I reflected on times I'd been out shopping for a product and took forever to decide on that one particular item. But once I finally made a decision and bought it, I found myself buying another eight items on the way out of the store. This phenomenon is common among consumers. Once the flow begins, the buyer becomes more open to making more purchases. It is my belief that the consumer is actually using the second and follow-up purchases to support the rightness of his first decision.

Why does someone refer you to his or her dentist? To help the dentist? Maybe, but more likely they've referred you because in convincing others to go to the same dentist it supports the rightness of their decision. Everyone wants to know they're doing the right thing and the other purchase phenomenon supports his actions and gives him the reassurance that what he did earlier was correct. Find one woman walking down Rodeo Drive in Beverly Hills, carrying just one shopping bag (if you can) and my entire theory is supported!

Another example of this is a customer who walks into a travel agency with the idea of taking a cruise. He spends four hours with the travel agent looking at all of the cruise line brochures while trying to figure out what package will best suit his needs. *Should I go take a cruise to Europe, Mexico, Alaska or the Caribbean? Should I take a five-day cruise or a two-week cruise? What is the best cruise line and who has the best ships?* Once the customer decides on a destination and purchases the perfect cruise vacation, the climate is right for the travel agent to step in and offer additional products. There's accommodation upgrades from an inside deck cabin to an ocean view suite, the island tour excursion package, travel insurance, airfare upgrades and on and on. Because the customer has taken the plunge and bought the first item, he's going to be right about his first decision, making him available to purchase additional products and services in order to support that initial decision.

I was raising money for my church and working on a prospect that had been very resistant to make any contributions. When I finally got him to agree to make a donation after much resistance, I congratulated him. As I watched him write the check I looked at him and said, "You know you're going to do more than that before you die. Your heart's in the right place. You're a generous man. Why don't you just do the rest now." He looked at me and said, "You're right." He tore up the first check and wrote me another for twenty times the amount that he'd initially decided on!

If you've ever seen someone at a restaurant complaining about the price of a steak, then turn around and order a bottle of wine that's twice the cost of the meal, you know what I'm talking about. How about the person who whines about paying ten bucks for a movie ticket and then spends another twenty on popcorn, soda and candy? Have you ever heard a guy complaining about how high his car payment is? This is the same guy who later customized the car with 22" wheels, a custom paint job and installed a stereo system that you can hear from three blocks away! Of course he had to charge it to his credit card at eighteen percent and the payments on the wheels, paint and audio amount to more than the payments on the car. *Yay for the second money! Learn this one and your life will change forever!*

The More They Spend the Better They Feel

Your prospect, regardless of what he says, always wants more, not less. Believe it or not, people love to spend money and the more money they spend, the more they enjoy spending it and the more they will enjoy their decision. Show me one person who has ever come in under their budget when buying a home, car furniture, equipment, clothes, a vacation or anything. They don't exist. Consumers want to take home lots of things, not just one thing. They want to brag to their friends and neighbors that they spent the most money and bought the most expensive thing. *People love showing off.* If they didn't there'd be no market for sports cars and designer clothing. Anyone can buy a leather purse that will last just as long as a designer handbag, but people know that the designer brand cost ten times more because of the label and insignia. This is America, a nation of consumers and one-uppers. Good or bad, we like to buy and we like to be seen buying. Therefore, the second purchase reinforces that the first purchase was the right decision.

Second money is easier to get than the first money. People will tell you, "Don't get greedy, don't complicate the close, just finish it or you might blow the deal with your attempts to get the second money." Nonsense. This kind of thinking is for the little, mediocre salespeople of the world, not for you! Second money is for those who want to take their game and their income to the next level and want to do it in half the time.

You'll spend ninety percent of your time eating the main course and ten percent eating the desert. Get the first sale wrapped up and then focus on the second sale—it's the dessert.

This is a monster technique that works like magic. All a salesperson has to do to unlock the door of second money is get over his own fear of blowing the deal by *asking* for it!

Remember, money is a mental issue, not a shortage issue.

Chapter Seven Questions:

If others have a difficult time getting money from you what will happen to you?

Write down some of the strange things you have done when it came time to part with your money:

1)

2)

3)

What is the easiest money there is to get and why?

Why would someone feel better if they spent more rather than less?

Why would money be a mental issue not a real shortage issue?

CHAPTER EIGHT

YOU ARE IN THE PEOPLE BUSINESS

The People Business Not the "X" Business

Manufacturers are constantly pushing product awareness and product knowledge because they believe this is the weakness of their sales force. They think if the salespeople just understood how the product worked and the benefits of it, they'd sell more. While it's true that salespeople must have a great understanding of their products, one must not forget that it's *people* who buy those products. That's why it's vital that salespeople know about people first, products second. I've known salespeople who understood the ins and outs of the product and every detail but are unable to close the deal as they have inferior understanding of people. Being superior in product knowledge but inferior regarding people knowledge equals minimal results.

If you understand the product before you understand people, you are putting the cart in front of the horse. Realize that you're in the people business first and the product business second. Certainly you need product knowledge. You have to know the benefits and how the product compares to others, but first and foremost, you need to understand people and what they want before you can sell the product or show someone the benefits of it.

Most salespeople I meet spend too much time selling the product and forget that selling is eighty-percent people and twenty-percent product. This is justified by people buying inferior products every minute of every day. Why is this? Because people buy for reasons other than just the product benefits.

A person stops into a convenience store after work and buys a carton of milk. Is that brand of milk the very best they can possibly drink? Is it the best price in town? That person doesn't know and doesn't care because it's not the carton of milk that they're buying. It's the convenience they're buying that will get them home to their family as quickly as possible.

The shoeshine guy at the airport does not understand that it's not the price or the quality of the shoeshine that keeps people from stopping at his booth. He does not realize this because he thinks he is shining shoes. The reason the businessman does not stop for a shoeshine is because he does not need a shine and not because of the cost. The business person is concerned about missing his connecting flight. If the shoeshine guy advertised: "Sixty-second Shines," he would have to expand his booth to handle all the business. To get the right button to close the sale, you have to know that you are in the people business, not the shoeshine business. Learn to think like they think. Products do not think, feel or react, people do.

I live in Los Angeles and my wife and I buy gas from a station on Sunset Boulevard where the owner comes out, greets us by name, fills the car up, cleans our windshields and gives us a bottle of water for free! Am I buying the gas or the service? Is this about people or the grade and quality of the fuel that is being put into my car? Is the owner selling people or gas? Where do you think we fill up? If you understand people, then you will get the right answer. The owner of the station understands that he is not in the gas business, he is in the people business which is why we continue to buy from him.

It has been said that people do not care how much you know until they know how much you care. I believe this is true and I can validate it with commission checks. I never consider that I am selling a product, but I do consider that I am helping a person make the right decision. I have sold fish, cars, clothes, real estate, videos, jewelry, investments and even ideas. I found that I did best when I was interested in the individual – the "human being" that wants to enjoy life and solve a problem by buying my product.

More often than not, salespeople launch into their pitch without ever knowing anything about the customer, which is a sure-fire way to miss the sale. What is important to the buyer? What does he need? What is the ideal scene for him? What is it they are actually trying to accomplish with a purchase? What is it that really makes them feel good? If they could get everything they wanted what would that be? These are the questions that will let you know how to sell them.

Take interest in the client instead of interest in selling him something. When a buyer goes out looking for a product he doesn't care how much you know about the product. He only cares about himself, his time, his money and doing the best thing for himself. He cares most about himself at this time, and you and your product are way down on his list of concerns.

The Most Interesting Person in the World

"I may not be the most interesting person, but I am the one I'm most interested with."

-- Anonymous

People are far more concerned and interested in themselves, their family and in doing the right thing than they are in having another product no matter how much they need or want it.

If you don't show as much interest in the buyer and his concerns as you do in selling, he'll know that you are only in it for the commission. Be more interested in the customer than you are in yourself, your sales process, your product or your commission and you will make more sales.

My wife and I recently met with a high-end, veteran real estate agent who was showing us a house. As we were walking through the property I began to tell the agent what was important to us at which point she cut me off and continued to pitch the house. You'd think that this agent was a rookie to the business, but on the contrary, she'd been in real estate for over twenty years. Maybe that was part of her problem. She had joined the ranks of those in the *real estate business* and had forgotten she was in the people business.

Ninety-percent of all salespeople don't take the

time to listen to the prospect or find out what they're actually looking for! While this agent has been very successful compared to others, imagine what that agent could sell if she was genuinely interested in people and in determining what they wanted and needed! It would certainly save her time as she would know what to show me and how to sell me. It's easy to do, but you have to be interested and you have to know how to communicate. Not talk, but communicate! True communication requires finding out what is important to people so you can identify what they actually want and then deliver that thing or things. What do people value? What is important? Why is it important? How do they want to be spoken to? What is going to cause them to take action?

One time I was selling a condominium to a couple in Tucson and I observed that the husband wouldn't look at me. After a couple of minutes I bluntly asked him, "Excuse me. Why won't you look at me?" He was shocked at first, but then started talking to me. I took interest in him, and when I did he started communicating with me. I asked him what his ideal scene was in a place to live. The question allowed him to open up and he told me everything they were looking for. During the conversation the subject of golf came up, so I showed him where the closest course was. He went on and on talking about golf and he didn't stop until he'd signed the documents. I barely even sold the condo; I just took interest in him, got into communication with him, made him more important than the product I was selling. I found out what was important to him, I listened and then I closed.

Communication = Sales

If you don't get into communication with the buyer you have no chance of ever making the sale. The dictionary defines communication as *a process in which information is exchanged between individuals through common symbols or behavior.*

Just talking about your product is not communicating because there's no exchange of ideas between you and the buyer. In sales we're interested in communication that gains access to information, which can be turned into action. To gain information means that your communication should include lots of questions. *"What do you want this product to do that your present one doesn't do for you? What would your present product have to do so that you would be satisfied with it? On a scale from one to ten, how would you rate what you are using / own now. What would make it a ten?"* This type of (interested in you) questioning will help you discover what the buyer wants, what they need and most importantly to what they assign value. Additionally, asking questions demonstrates your interest in the individual and people want to know you are interested in them, not just in a sale.

Years ago I was shopping for a computer and the salesperson started reeling off about the speed, the memory and storage capacity, the megabytes and all this technical information that meant nothing to me. I walked away from him feeling like a zombie from all of the technological terms and misunderstandings that he spewed at me, and I didn't make a purchase. A week later I wandered into another store and met a real salesperson who approached me and immediately started asking me questions rather than spewing data. He asked me if I'd be traveling with the computer and what the three main uses would be to determine how I would be using it and what would make it valuable to me. That salesperson showed more interest in me in sixty seconds than the other guy did in fifteen minutes. He was also genuinely interested in finding the right product for me rather than making a sale. I told him that I'd been considering buying a particular model to which he promptly explained that the computer I was considering was more than I actually needed and I'd wind up spending more than necessary. His helpful advice increased my trust, putting him in the position to control the sale and keep me interested.

I wound up buying two laptops and a desktop computer from him in less than twenty minutes. Before I left, I asked him what else I might need and then purchased extra memory cards, software programs and extended warranties. The first guy took fifteen minutes demonstrating his product knowledge, but he didn't bother to find out about me and didn't get the sale. Why? He put product knowledge before people knowledge. The guy who sold me the product and got the commission also knew product knowledge and that was essential for him to guide me to the right product. But he didn't put the product knowledge first. He put me first. The human quality involved in selling can never be replaced and becomes even more beneficial the more deeply we become entrenched in the machine age.

I want to clarify: when I suggest you ask questions it is not done with the intent of manipulation. This has been greatly misused by sales trainers over the years. Questions are asked to find out more about helping the human being in front of you rather than to manipulate.

Many books regarding sales suggest a tactic of collecting information to use against the buyer later. There are even tricks suggesting that the salesperson doesn't answer questions, but that he responds to the buyer's questions with more questions. That is manipulation, not communication with the intent of helping and will not serve you over time.

I'm in the people business, not the product business and certainly not in the business of manipulation.

People are Senior to Products (Critical for Executives)

Make this a fundamental rule you live and die by: you are in the people business not the product business. People are senior to the products! People are senior to the processes employed by companies. No product or sales process will ever be successful if it doesn't make people senior! A product is dead, people are not. A process is a function and always less important than people. To the degree that a company's sales process becomes more important than the people that process will fail.

A personal friend of mine and rookie commercial real estate agent asked me for a meeting about an investment property I was considering. I won't mention the name of the company he worked for, but I can tell you that they're one of the largest firms in the world representing apartment buildings and they rely on a very stringent sales process.

I told my friend to come to my house for a meeting. He told me it was essential that I come into his office rather than him coming to see me. I thought this was strange and told him, "Just meet me at my office and let's figure out how I can buy something from you." He called me back and insisted that I come to his office! This was totally uncharacteristic of my friend. I asked him why he continued to insist on this because there was no way I was going down to his office and that if he wanted to meet with me he'd have to come to my home or not meet with me at all. At this point he agreed. When he finally got to my home we sat at my kitchen table and I asked him why he continued to persist that I come to his office. He explained that he'd been to a seminar and the company's sales approach *insisted* on the client going into their office. This was a "control" point that the company promoted to their young salespeople, suggesting they would be able to control the client and get more listings.

While it's vital to have a sales process in place, the moment the process becomes senior to servicing the customer it will always err! This particular process failed to include me, the buyer! By the way, my friend never sold me any real estate. Instead, he quit his job at that company after I convinced him to come and work with me managing my property. This proved to be a very successful decision for both of us. He went on to become a prosperous business owner and real estate entrepreneur. To this day he thanks me for not meeting him at his office! People are senior to processes.

I remember when the Hummer H2 first came out. I was so excited after I'd seen one that I immediately called up a Hummer dealership because I wanted to buy one. I didn't need a Hummer, but I wanted one, and I wanted it now! A salesperson answered the phone and I asked how much a Hummer was. He told me that he couldn't give me a price over the phone. I asked if there was something wrong with him because I'd just called for a price and he'd stated that he couldn't tell me. He said it was a company policy not to give prices over the phone. Wow! What a policy! This Hummer dealership has a policy in place that prevents people from purchasing anything! He then told me that the policy was there to prevent people from shopping price over the phone and going to a competitor. I hadn't even been thinking about shopping a competitor until he planted the seed in my mind. *"Hmmm. Maybe I should shop the price..."* I wondered why the Hummer dealership bothered to advertise their phone number if they weren't willing to answer questions.

This is a perfect example of a business that has implemented poor policy in an effort to prevent people from shopping competitors. Some genius in management came up with a policy that not only prevents people from buying, but also makes no sense to the buyer and probably no sense to the salesperson. This results in a complete waste of advertising dollars, creates a confrontational environment, destroys sales and creates high turnover.

Processes put in place without considering the effect on the customer will be ineffective and destructive. People are always going to be more important than processes, procedures or policies.

People write checks; policies and processes don't. Products are dead matter and people are alive. Products can be replaced, but people can not be. Products don't sell themselves, but people do. Never forget, people buy products and it's your job to sell people on your product, not to sell your product to people.

Caring about people is senior to the products and the processes you use. Be genuinely concerned that your customer is getting the right product for them. Make the individual more important than the individual sale and you'll make more sales. Be interested in what the person is trying to accomplish and what problem he's trying to solve and treat people as individuals, as living breathing individuals that are irreplaceable. Stay interested before the sale, during the sale and after the sale and even if you don't get the sale. Don't ever let the process be senior to the people!

You're not in the real estate business, mortgage business, insurance business, investing business, newspaper business, clothing business, acting business, hotel business, seminar business or whatever "business" your industry calls itself. Quit the business you think you're in right now and get into the *people business!*

Chapter Eight Questions:

While it is important to be an expert on your product, why is it more important to become a people expert?

What is the 80/20 Rule?

What are people most interested in?

Any questions? Call 800-368-5771

What is the most important part of the definition regarding communication?

Write three examples of how to get someone to exchange communication with you:

What one thing should always be kept senior to the product, policy or the process?

THE MAGIC OF AGREEMENT

Always Agree With the Customer

ALWAYS, ALWAYS, ALWAYS agree with the customer.

This is the single most important and the most commonly violated rule in all of selling! If you want *agreement,* you've got to be *agreeable* with your customers.

This vital rule is not to be confused with the old saying, *the customer is always right* because customers aren't always right. If you've ever been with one, you know what I'm talking about. The point is, right or wrong, agree with the customer. Agree as you write the deal, don't disagree and fight the deal!

You can never expect someone to agree with you if you're disagreeing with them. It will almost never happen. People are attracted to products, ideas and people that represent the things they're in agreement with. This is a fact of the universe! Your friends are those people that most agree with your core beliefs. Your favorite family members are the people you want to spend your time with during the holidays. These are the people in your life that you've got the most agreement with. People that agree with one another move toward each other and people that disagree move apart. The common saying that "opposites attract" doesn't happen to be true in sales. In selling, likes attract and like is born out of agreement. I like you because I agree with you at some level.

It Only Takes One

When there's not enough agreement between two parties, there's no agreement at all. This is the reason that partnerships fail, marriages break up and why you don't have more customers buying from you. Most people think that it takes two to have an agreement. But the truth is, it only takes one to agree, because once one opposing party agrees, there is no longer any disagreement. The salesperson who wants agreement must give agreement to the customer before agreement can be achieved. Even when a buyer is making ridiculous claims or exaggerations, agree with him. Just because you think what he's saying is ridiculous doesn't mean he thinks it's ridiculous. If he thinks something is black and you think it's white, you're both right. However, if he thinks something is black and you want to get the sale, you'd better agree with his reality that it's black. If he thinks he should wait and think about it and you disagree with him, you'll solidify his need to wait and never get him to close. However, if you were to simply agree with him that thinking about it is a good idea and let him know that you agree, he'll be more attracted to you and move toward you not away from you. Once you've agreed with him, you can go ahead and explain that thinking will not change the fact that this is the right product, that he can afford the product, that his company will save money because of the product, and by making a decision to do it now he can put his attention on all the other things he has to think about. Agree with him first which will bring him up to another way of thinking.

I wanted to add a fourth dog to our family and my wife was dead set against the idea. The first thing I did was agree with her. "You're right honey. The last thing we need is another Great Dane."

With a raised eyebrow, she asked, "You agree with me?"

"Absolutely I agree," I professed. "You're right. There's no sense in us having four dogs."

That was the point where she looked at the picture of the puppy and a little smile crossed her lips. "He is so cute."

Done! Dog number four is in the house! Do you get it? Agree, acknowledge, make the other party right and then close the deal.

There is no single rule that salespeople violate more than this one, and it happens to be the number one rule in selling any product. AGREEING IS THE ROAD TO MORE SALES! This needs to be drilled and practiced because man is inclined to disagree in order to satisfy his gluttonous craving to be right.

The Agreement Challenge

You have to really practice this and it's best if you practice with a friend, family member or work associate. You can even record different scenarios into a digital recorder and practice handling them whereby you agree first, then handle.

This is the drill. Try to agree with everyone you talk to for a single day. Try this around the house as you're given endless opportunities everyday to do the exact opposite of what I'm asking you to do in this drill. I'll bet you can't even make it through one day without violating this very vital and basic rule of selling. Try it! If you find yourself disagreeing outwardly with any person then start over until you can get through a whole day agreeing with everyone.

I know people that started this exercise at 8:00 AM and by 8:30 AM had already failed.

Your kid says he doesn't want to go to school today. Handle him by agreeing first. "I understand what you're saying because I didn't want to go to school on Fridays either. Now get dressed my little buddy and let's get to school."

Your husband wants to go see a new action movie, but you'd rather go out for a romantic dinner. Agree first. "You're right. It's a great night for a movie. Why don't we go down to that new café first and get a bite to eat?" Once you've agreed, it's possible to suggest alternatives that are more suitable for you. Now that you're at the café, you'll either learn to sell him on something else or have to go to the action movie. Either way you are going to spend time with your spouse and both of you win.

A client tells you, "It's too much money." Now it's for real! "I agree it's a lot of money. Everyone that invests in this product agrees that this system is a big investment when they're buying it. That's why you should get it installed so that it can start making you money right away."

"A new roof is a lot of money," the customer objects. "I agree it's a lot of money. Your new roof is going to last for thirty years and there won't be anymore leaks or costly repairs. You will have to do it sooner or later, lets get it done now."

"The bedrooms are too small," the buyer says. "You're right," you agree. "That's one of the first things I noticed too. What do you think can be done about it?"

Agree and then offer the buyer an opportunity to find the solution before you offer one to find out how much of an objection it actually is.

"We never make a rash decision!" the customer says. "And I agree with you," you say. "To make a rash decision would be the wrong thing to do and I wouldn't want you to do that. However, you have been thinking about upgrading for sometime now. You've used the same computer system for ten years and it's time to update it. If you would have done it nine years ago, it would have been rash, but now it just makes sense."

The ability to agree with the customer is senior to all other rules in selling! Agreement is even senior to closing the deal. I can't believe I'm saying that because I see the close as something SACRED. However, if you disagree with someone before the close, you risk never getting to the point where you can close. Show me the top one-percent of all salespeople in any industry and I'll show you people who are masters at agreeing with their customers first and closing them later on what they wanted all along.

Salespeople are constantly trying to sell and negotiate by disagreement. This is no different than trying to swim against the current. In most cases the person doesn't drown from water in his lungs, he drowns from exhaustion fighting against the water itself. Most salespeople drown in the negotiations from exhaustion of trying to overcome every objection. Start the sale from agreement, continue to agree, make the buyer right – close later.

You're right! I'm with you! I agree! Let me see what I can do for you! I understand! I will make that happen! Done!

Regardless of how off-key or incorrect the buyer may be, it's critical that the relationship is built on agreement if you want to make the sale.

Some people will say that agreeing when you don't really agree is manipulation. While I'm willing to agree with them that they see it as manipulation, I see agreeing as my attempt to get along. I think that disagreeing with people manipulates you out of a sale and that doesn't make sense. If you say it's hot and I think it's cold, I'm able to agree with your *viewpoint* that you think it's hot. What have I lost? I'm simply acknowledging that you think it's hot. This is not manipulation, but understanding. You didn't ask me what I thought. All I did was agree with your reality without adding that I think it's cold which would only serve to make you wrong. By establishing basic agreement, you're creating the opportunity to help the buyer purchase your product or service. If the buyer never gets a chance to see what you're offering because of an earlier disagreement, then know that you've made an error by not allowing them to see your product or service in the proper light. All you've done is put their focus on the disagreement rather than on your product.

How to Soften Any Buyer

Let's say a customer tells you they've only got ten minutes and you know you can't do your presentation in ten minutes. I've watched salespeople spend ten minutes talking about how they can't do the presentation that quickly. A better alternative is agree that ten minutes would be fine and go right into your presentation. If you start the relationship off with agreement, you'll have a chance to tell the prospect about your product. Additionally, you'll come across as understanding, easy to deal with and professional.

I've been in hundreds of selling situations where the entire process started off with the buyer limiting the amount of time I had. I love this because I immediately tell them the time they offered me is more than enough. By the customer's response you'd think I'd just stepped into a phone booth and flew out with a cape on. The buyer looks at me like I am SUPER SALESPERSON and they immediately know they're dealing with a professional. Customers respect me because of the fact that I agreed, not because I was slick at handling their objections. What created this response or change in the buyer? It wasn't some tricky, manipulative line. It was because I agreed to their limitations and I was willing to work with what time they'd offered me. I showed them my appreciation instead of voicing disagreement. I'd rather have ten minutes than no minutes! By first agreeing with them, you can then move on with your presentation. Nothing will soften a buyer more than being agreeable.

The Magic Words

Regardless of whether the customer is right or wrong, you need to make it safe for him to be right so he doesn't get so stuck in his "rightness" that he's unable to change his mind.

If you want people to agree with your viewpoint,

all you've got to do is agree with their position, agree with their opinions and step into their shoes for a moment.

If you want to keep an argument going with someone, tell them that they're wrong. If you want to keep a raving maniac going on and on about how right he is, just disagree with him. If you want to get him to shut up, agree with him and he'll stop behaving like a raving maniac.

There's no easier way to instantly end an argument than by agreeing with the opposition. A friend of mine who'd been married for seventeen years said that the magic formula to her relationship was telling her husband, "You're right." Who can argue with that? By ending silly arguments, one can move on and enjoy the important things in life.

Customer service problems can be handled the same way. When you get a complaint, go ahead and agree with the complaint. "You guys screwed everything up!" the customer shouts. "I agree with you sir," you say, "Let me figure out how to correct it for you." But if you tell him he's wrong, you're only adding gasoline to his fire of disagreements.

You've probably experienced this phenomenon in your life. As an exercise, try it with your spouse or a friend. Wait until they say something and then tell them they're wrong. Watch what happens.

You've just fueled an argument. To end off on the argument, tell them they're right! By agreeing, you cool off and put out the fire of disagreement. End of argument!

I once told a salesperson that I wanted to pay cash for the product at which time he said, "You don't want to pay cash for it, you should finance it." This created a block to my power of decision and lessened my enthusiasm for continuing to do business with him. By disagreeing with me, the salesperson created a barrier to what should have been an easy sale. He could have simply said, "Cash would be great sir." Then, as he was taking my cash, he could have shown me both the cash price and the alternative if I financed, at which point I would have at least considered the alternative as a choice, not a "make wrong."

Agreement is the fastest route to getting your way! Do yourself a favor and practice agreeing with people. The three most powerful words in the English language are "YOU ARE RIGHT!" And the two most powerful words in the English language are "I AGREE!"

Agreeing with the customer means control for the salesperson, happier customers and quicker decisions. Miracles take place out of agreement.

Chapter Nine Questions:

What is the first rule of selling?

How many people does it take to resolve a conflict?

To get an agreement, you must first do what?

www.grantcardone.com

Write responses to the following (then look at how I handled it):

"It's too much money"

"A new roof is a lot of money"

"The bedrooms are too small"

"We never make rash decisions"

ESTABLISHING TRUST

Show, Don't Tell

In this chapter you'll discover how you can earn and secure full trust with your buyer and in so doing increase your effectiveness.

Because of a handful of unethical salespeople who have misrepresented the benefits of their products, customers may not completely trust everything you tell them. TV news broadcasts and papers are constantly running stories about scams and cons that make consumers skeptical of salespeople. This skepticism keeps the prospect on guard and prevents the sales person from correctly establishing the trust that is critical to getting a decision.

Regardless of the cause, it's critical that you're aware of the buyer's lack of trust and that you tackle it. Distrust in the sales cycle is not the buyer's problem but yours! If the buyer doesn't trust you or your presentation then the information that you're offering will be minimized, challenged or shopped. Of course, the buyer will make a decision; it just won't be the one you want. When the buyer decides to "think about it," that's a decision, but unfortunately not the one you were looking for.

A salesperson always gets a decision from the customer, always! They decided to think about it and you got them to do that! You convinced them to go home and talk about it. They decided to present it to the board. That was all because of you!

When the buyer doesn't trust the salesperson or something about the presentation they'll add time to the cycle by *not* making a decision to purchase. Even if you manage to close the deal, the unhandled element of distrust will almost always guarantee future problems in delivering and servicing the buyer.

When a salesperson understands what's going on in the mind of his customer he's just stepped into an area that only a professional would delve into. The unspoken thoughts of the customer is an interesting field where we are no longer looking at what the buyer said, but what he *didn't say*. We're looking at what's going on behind the scenes in the customer's mind. When a salesperson is willing to go there, that's the point where he transitions from a painter to an artisan! All my studies in sales over the last twenty-five years have involved the mind of the customer, not just his money.

Prospects Don't Make Sales, Salespeople Do

As stated earlier, prospects do not stop sales, the salesperson stops the sale. Understand also that prospects do not make sales either. It is the salesperson's job to make the sale. Whether or not the sale happens is entirely up to you, not the prospect.

In order to make sales, you have to understand the mind of the customer. If you don't recognize how buyers think and what causes them to respond and act, you'll be unable to take full responsibility and will never reach your full potential. When you step into this arena you are now in the business of handling people, not products. People are run by their minds. Understand the mind and you understand people.

Most salespeople tend to blame their customers when sales are down, but they don't usually do so to the customer's face. They do it later when they're with their co-workers. *"He can't make a decision. He doesn't know what he wants. He wants more than he can afford. He's just wasting my time."* On and on! I never tolerate this sort of talk from any of the people that work with me. This unwanted behavior is an indication of very low responsibility, and low responsibility = No sale.

The salesperson must assume responsibility for himself, the prospect and all that occurs.

One time a buyer in a retail furniture store said to me, "I'm not buying anything today." With a smile I replied, "Sir if you don't buy anything today it'll be my fault, not yours." He looked at me with a grin and said, "Great. Let me tell you what I'm looking for." The customer *did* buy from me that day and we furnished his entire house. All I did was take full responsibility for the selling *and the buying*. Also, I understood that him saying he wasn't buying was just a reactive response from his mind and not really *him*. The only thing the buyer should ever have to do is give you the money.

The buyer who states, "I'm not buying today," indicates his lack of trust of either salespeople or his ability to make good decisions. It's vital that you understand why the buyer is wary of salespeople and why he distrusts his own ability to make decisions. These points must be understood and handled.

When someone meets you and you sense his or her distrust, know that it doesn't have anything to do with you personally. You haven't even said anything yet! Perhaps the blue shirt you're wearing reminded him of some bad experience he had. I don't know, but I do know that if you don't handle it, you will not sell him!

Credibility = Increased Sales

A lack of trust will cost you sales! Distrust will cost you credibility and lost credibility will add time and reduce your chances at the sale.

Credibility is one of the most valuable assets you have as a salesperson. When something happens that puts your credibility into question, it becomes difficult to get the buyer to trust his decision to do business with you. If an element of distrust exists, no matter what you say or how you beg, plead or persuade, realize that you've got your hands full and you must handle the distrust first in order to get the job done. You must rebuild your credibility immediately. Ignoring the credibility issue won't make it disappear. It has to be handled! When the buyer doesn't trust, you can use all of the greatest closing lines throughout history and watch them fall upon deaf ears.

Great salespeople understand the buyer's distrust, accept full responsibility for it and never take it personally.

I always assume that the buyer doesn't trust a single word I say to them. They might not even believe that my name is what I say it is which is why wearing a nametag is a great idea. A nametag creates something that they know they can trust because they can see it. When I'm talking about the product, I provide everything I say in writing or support it with printed materials. If I'm telling a buyer that the piece of property is 44,000 square feet, I'll show them the documentation that supports my statement and this will start to show the prospect that I'm trustworthy, that I know what I am doing and he'll lend credibility to what I say in the future!

People Believe What They See, Not What They Hear

Have you ever noticed that a buyer isn't fully listening to you? This phenomenon occurs because the buyer assumes that he can't trust what a salesperson says.

People believe what they see, not what they hear. Always have your presentation, proposals and prices in writing for the buyer so they can see it with their own eyes.

Your prospect will not believe words he hears, but will believe the words they can see. Tell a guy some unbelievable and bizarre conspiracy theory that you heard about and then show him the article where you read it. If it's in writing it becomes more real to him.

I had a very wealthy friend and I wanted to get him to invest with me on a real estate deal. I didn't tell him a single thing about the property, the deal or the investment. I didn't waste one second telling him how good the investment was since he has been told this a thousand times. I called him and asked him to meet me at the property because I wanted to get his opinion about how I could expand my company and wanted him to see what I was doing so he could give me the best advice. I *showed* him the properties, the tenants, the competition, the possibilities. Within thirty minutes of touring just one of the projects he was asking if he could invest in the project!

I want you to make this a rule that you sell by: *assume that your buyer, no matter how well you know the person, never believes your words and will only believe that which you can show them.*

As I stated earlier, there are many reasons for distrust and it's necessary that you know what they are. The most common and least considered is the buyer's own experience with fabrications, exaggerations and embellishments. You've got to assume that at some point in his life, he committed such an offense himself. It might be something major or it might be something minor like the time he lied to his parents about not feeling good so he didn't have to go to school. Whatever it was, the buyer knows that another person is capable of slight exaggerations or even outright lies because *he's done so himself.* The buyer believes that if he's done this, then you'll do it too even if you won't! Regardless of how honest you are and how much integrity you might have, your prospect believes that you're capable of the same things he has been guilty of. This belief and distrust is what is real to that person, regardless of how much you try to convince him otherwise.

The element of distrust is intensified when your prospect has had the negative experience of being ripped-off by some earlier salesperson or by a time when he had a plain misunderstanding between what was said and what was promised. People have misunderstandings all the time and misunderstandings can lead to distrust. I want you to try this simple exercise to prove my point. Write down a short story about something that happened to you and read that story to one person and have that person pass it on verbally to another person and continue this until at least five people hear the story. Have the last person come back and tell you what they were told and compare it to what you wrote down. I assure that your story will have changed and the story didn't change because of lies, but because of incorrect duplication and misunderstandings. If you had passed your story in writing to each person there would have been a greatly reduced chance of misunderstandings.

How to Handle the Buyer's Distrust

The rule to handle a buyer's distrust is to always use and show written material to support your presentation and proposal. When you're documenting facts for your customer, it's preferable to use third party materials that support what you're saying. Remember, people believe what they see not what they hear.

Always, always, always write down what you've said, offered, proposed, promised, implied and suggested. Anytime you're going for the close, insist on putting it in writing.

I see so many salespeople shying away from contracts, buyer's orders and signatures! Why? Because they falsely believe that they may scare the customer with a pen or a contract. This is a ridiculous assumption that has no basis in reality.

You don't go into a military operation without equipment and supplies and you never go for the close without a pen and a contract! There's nothing to hide. You aren't a covert operation or some kind of criminal that needs to sneak around. You are a professional salesperson offering a product that will benefit and solve problems for your prospect when they purchase and own it.

When you're presenting your product write it down or show them the benefits on paper. If you're showing them how your product will improve their business, show them the proof by statistics and success stories. I used to keep an evidence manual with me to show my facts and what others had said as a result of doing business with me. People love to see that you are prepared and sold on your product.

When you show them what your competition will do or will not do, prove it in writing. When you know you've got the best price, the best product and the best service, always back it up with documentation. If you do this satisfactorily, you'll earn trust and reduce the prospect's need to shop, think, research and talk to others, all the while increasing your odds of closing the sale.

It's incredible how much significance people place on the written word and you want to capitalize on it. Every day, people quote things that they read in the paper without ever researching it for themselves. They assume that if it was written it must be true! People read books in school and then go through the rest of their lives believing it was true. Twenty years ago a book was written and the first line read, "Life is difficult." This book became a best seller and everyone adopted this one line as truth, when it was garbage. That line certainly isn't true to me and it's definitely not a quote that I'd live my life by. But because it was written, people assumed it was true and adopted it as their own reality.

Newspapers perpetuate things that are not true and history books are filled with errors, opinions, false reports, agendas and even outright lies. Some of the best-known books were written many years after the events even took place and long after all of the players were dead. Yet if it is written people tend to believe it is true! Remember the movie, Jerry McGuire where the character played by Cuba Gooding Jr. kept saying to the Tom Cruise character, "Show me the money!" In sales, the customer is Cuba screaming, "Show me the data!" That's the point here, show the proof to the prospect, make it real to him and he'll have the confidence to buy.

With the abundance of information available today through third parties, consumer guides, the Internet and other sources, your prospect becomes even more dependent on facts to support decisions. Buyers are going to continue to rely on these sources, so you need to make use of those same sources to support your cause and help the buyer make the right decision.

Any time you're presenting product information, performance reports, facts, historical data, comparison information, pricing data, proposals, etc., the rule is *don't tell, show.* The automotive industry is notorious for not wanting to give information to prospects and because of this error the industry suffers from high turnover, poor loyalty, high advertising costs and shrinking profits. The premise was, "The less they know the better off we are!" Nothing could be further from the truth. The more the buyer knows, the more they can trust the information and the more likely they are to buy. By offering written information, your sales will be easier, you'll make more money and you'll have more satisfied customers.

As a salesperson, I prefer informed buyers over uninformed buyers for the very reason that an informed buyer can make a decision and can be handled with logic while the uninformed buyer cannot make a decision and tends to get emotional. When facts, data and logic are missing people get emotional, and when people get emotional they can get irrational. It's okay to sell with emotion, but you want to close with logic, data and facts. An informed professional buyer is much easier to sell than one that is not. Someone who is not informed about the product will make an offer that has no reality involved in it. That would be an emotional offer, not a logical one. I want logic and facts in the close, not emotions. So I keep people logical by providing them with credible validation they can trust.

Tips on Using Written and Visual Information to Close:

- Never sell with words, always show documentation.

- Never negotiate with words; write your

negotiations down on paper.

- Never ask for the close with words. Use a buyer's order.

- Never make verbal promises. Put your assurances in writing.

- The more data, the better. Don't be afraid to use a lot of data.

- Keep your information current.

- Have your written information available and easy to access.

- Use third party data as much as possible.

- The more you're able to access the data in real time the better. Real time data is preferable to prepared data.

- Use computer generated data whenever possible!

- Have Internet access available so you can pull the data up in front of the customer and they can see that it hasn't been contrived or manipulated.

Make it easy for the buyer to do research while they're with you instead of at home or at their office when you can't be there. If the buyers want to look up their own information or research, encourage them to do so.

After consulting thousands of companies on improving their sales processes, I've often encouraged business, management and salespeople to make all competitive advertising available and fully displayed in their offices so that the buyer doesn't have to go out and look at what the competition is offering but can do so without leaving.

Help 'em Believe You

People want to believe you, but you have to help them. If you have a good product and a good service then do everything you can to build your case and do it with written information. That way the buyer doesn't have to trust you. Once they read that what you're saying is so, they have no choice but to believe you.

I was involved in selling a 144-condo unit project that I owned and the onsite management was having trouble selling the units. I decided to visit the building and find out what was going on. So I walked into the office and asked them to run me through the process like I was a prospect. I found that there was no place to sign in and the pricing wasn't available because the pricing sheets were kept in another office. They weren't able to quote me a payment and finance rates and there was no data available to explain what the product offered. There was no competitive pricing displayed and there was nothing to offset the bad news about the neighborhood in the local newspapers.

Any questions? Call 800-368-5771

I fired the project managers and installed a new group of inexperienced, but eager people and made sure that they had everything available for the sales team and prospects to look at. We sold thirty units in three months. That was three times the sales that the previous people had made in a year.

Some people distrust the selling profession because of the actions of a few criminals and the inactions of many good intentioned salespeople who didn't understand this basic rule of selling: *people believe what they see, not what they hear.* So show them, don't tell them!

Chapter Ten Questions:

Three reasons people don't trust sales people as suggested by the author:

1)

2)

3)

Whose problem is it to handle the customer's distrust?

When your prospect doesn't fully trust the sales person or the presentation, what will they add to the cycle?

Give an example when you didn't trust either the sales person or the presentation and added time to the decision?

What is one of the most valuable assets of a sales person?

The author suggest that people believe what they see, not what they hear. Explain:

What are some ways the author suggests building trust?

1)

2)

3)

4)

GIVE, GIVE, GIVE

The Magic of Give, Give, Give

Selling is the act of giving not getting, serving not selling. Unfortunately, most people in sales are looking for their commission and what they're going to get out of the deal, rather than what they're going to give, what their product really offers and how the client will benefit. The old adage is that it's better to give than to receive, but in selling the only way to receive is to give first.

I believe that the true essence of selling is not just getting the sale, but the sincere desire to help. I also believe that a spiritually aware person will ultimately be a better salesperson than someone just interested in compensation.

I believe and have validated in my life that if you give enough in life, life will give back to you. It's the same in sales as it is in life. I don't mean giving the lowest price, or giving products and services away for free, but giving the most attention, the most energy, the best attitude, and the highest level of service.

Give, give, give is the assurance of sales, sales, sales. If your client wants one option, give them three or six or even twelve options.

I created a software program for retailers based on the Give, Give, Give philosophy. The program is called Epencil™ and provides the client with multiple options on different products in a succinct and professional manner. Epencil™ has been extremely successful in the auto industry where, for years, they were inclined not to give information or gave limited information. What I introduced was a program that when customers ask for information, they're given an array of payments, package options and price information, thereby making the buyer feel serviced not sold. This concept of taking give-give-give to an actual application resulted in increased profits, increased sales and happier customers for auto dealers. It fully utilizes the idea that service is senior to selling, and giving is senior to getting.

If someone asks me for a drink I get it for them, open the bottle, bring them a glass, ice and a napkin. That is give, give, give in action. I don't ask them if they want the glass and the ice - I deliver it and leave it to them whether they want it in the bottle or want me to pour it over ice! If I'm a waiter, I don't ask if you want desert after dinner. I *bring* you the desert tray, tell you about each desert, tell you about my favorite and dare you to pass. I can service you into the desert without ever looking like I was selling it!

A friend told me a story that illustrates the give, give, give attitude. She and her husband were leaving a restaurant in New Orleans one evening. As they walked out onto the street a haggard looking man in a threadbare coat approached them. He immediately approached them and asked the husband for permission to serenade his wife. Reluctantly, the husband agreed and the man got down on his knees before her right on the sidewalk and began singing. She said that the incredible voice and heart-felt passion that came from that desperate character was powerful enough to blow the glass out of every window on the block. The man went on singing for two minutes, pouring his heart and soul into that song and giving them every fiber of his being. When he finished, they were speechless. Her husband handed the guy $100. With tears of gratitude, the man thanked them then ran down the street to a beat up car where inside his wife and children were waiting. The only thing that the guy had to offer was his voice and he knew that if he didn't give it right then and there, his family wasn't going to eat that night. My friend's husband, a career salesman, said that he'd been so impressed by the man's intention to give that he hardly felt $100 was enough for what he received. That man on the street poured his soul into that song with the give, give, give attitude not knowing if the couple would even tip him at all. Regardless, for those two brief minutes he belonged entirely and completely to them.

Give all of you to a prospect, not just a part of you. Give all of your attention, all of your energy, all of your suggestions, all of your information and then find some more of you to give! Exceed expectations and go all the way with them and then a bit further. Withhold none of you and give yourself without reservation.

As a customer or client I don't want to have to ask a salesperson for something. I want him to offer it. I want him to predict what I need and offer it to me. I want to be provided with what I asked for and everything else that will help me to make a decision. This shows me that he wants to take care of me, is thinking like me and is actually predicting my expectations and surpassing them all at the same time. Deal closed!

Love the One You're With

Always pay attention to your customer and stay with them from start to finish without allowing interruptions. Show them how important they are to you and how they're the most important person in your universe. If you can do that you will be rewarded. If you chase two rabbits at the same time, both will get away. Commit to the one you're with all the way. Handle your phone calls and emails later and never allow interruptions.

Make your total commitment to that one opportunity, that one customer and let them know that! Give them all of you and they'll see that you're with them all the way. Regardless of them taking calls, or being interrupted, keep your focus on the person you're with. Too often, people feel neglected in life; so don't let them have that experience with you. Show them complete attention from beginning to end! Give, give, give your full, undivided attention to your customer and don't stop until you bring it home!

Make it your goal to give 100% of your attention to the customer regardless of the quality or estimated odds of closing the deal. Human beings are much more valuable than money. Treat them like that and you'll be rewarded.

In the business of sales, you have to be willing to serve people, not just sell them. For a business to survive and prosper it has to serve and help people, not just sell products. That means taking take care of customers and going beyond their expectations. The best salespeople I've ever met were not the fast talking guys, but the most service oriented. Those professionals that care the most are the ones who go the extra mile to find ways to improve the customer's life.

Are You a Holiday Inn or a Ritz Carleton?

As a salesperson, are you a Holiday Inn or a Ritz Hotel? Be honest with yourself and you'll see why you're being paid whatever you're currently making. If most of your customers are grinding you on price, then your level of service is not obvious to them otherwise they wouldn't grind you on just the price as they would value the service you give them.

One time I had 1700 apartments for sale. I had real estate agents lined up around the block begging for the listing, but none of them got it because I didn't trust they would service me the way I wanted. I gave it to the guy that I knew, trusted and actually paid him double what I would have paid any other agency. I chose him because I truly believed that I could count on him to give me the best advice and the best service. The agent that I chose was someone I believed in and I was willing to pay extra for it! Why would I do that? Because like most people, I don't want the best deal, I want the best service, the best product and the best representation. I want to know that you're going to be there for me no matter what. I want to know that there's not going to be unnecessary drama and conflict, and if there is, I want to know that you'll handle it.

Selling is about helping people, not just selling them. If you like helping people and perfect the other points I'm suggesting to you here, you will be great. Many salespeople whom I've met, who otherwise could have been great salespeople, have unfortunately been corrupted by others and led them to believe that they should rely on trickery and deception. You don't have to trick or deceive to sell. You have to be willing to serve and help people before you'll get the close. The more you're able to demonstrate that service-oriented attitude the easier your job will be. And trust me, no matter how much you serve someone you'll still have to be prepared to ask, "Will that be cash, check or credit card?"

Service is the only way to higher prices and less competition. A salesperson caught in a constant price conflict will never agree with my point because they're stuck in price as the solution. But price is not the solution; it never has been and never will be. Service is the solution! A better product is not the solution because sooner or later someone will have similar or better products and will sell them at a lower price.

A buyer will pay extra for great service, a great

attitude, ease of purchase, convenience and when they feel special. Look at how you can create a level of service that separates you from others. Going to the client rather than the client going to you is service. Providing options is a way to service a customer. Sending gifts, flowers, notes or just dropping by to say hello is service. A big smile, full attention and a great attitude are service. There's no real value in lower prices. What do I get for a lower price? I get a lower price and less service. I can get a room at a Holiday Inn for a fraction of the price of a room at the Ritz. What do I get for saving $400? I get a cheaper room, minimal service and "I don't care" attitudes. What is the difference between a five hundred dollar room and an eighty-dollar room? Service!

You don't have to look far to find companies that are known for great service and higher prices. People even brag that they pay extra to do business with them. Look at Tiffany's, Ritz Hotels, The Four Seasons and American Express Centurion. There are high-end beauty shops where haircuts are $700. But they aren't selling haircuts, they're giving service in abundance.

This kind of service is no different for a salesperson. If you elevate your level of service above the rest of the market, your customers will quit shopping the price. How much are you willing to bend over backwards to make sure your customer is happy?

Any questions? Call 800-368-5771

I attended a seminar once as a salesperson, and the speaker said that one should never call and ask the client how the product was working because it opens the conversation to problems. While the audience agreed I sat there in absolute disagreement. *If my customer is having a problem then I want to know about it so I can handle it.* Problems and dissatisfaction are opportunities for me to shine, for me to separate myself and to sell again. It's not a service department's problem, it's my customer's problem, and I want to take care of it for them.

Tip: Problem = Opportunities for Future <u>Sales</u>.

Service is Senior to Selling

No amount of slick advertising or Public Relations can replace poor service. Twice a year my wife and I go shopping for new clothes and one time we decided to go to a big department store in our neighborhood where they'd recently started promoting their new image of personal service and customer satisfaction. After twenty minutes of walking into this store, not a single person had greeted us. Not even a hello! It was unbelievable. We were two qualified buyers with the intent to buy something and there was no one willing to help us or even acknowledge that we were there. What were these people thinking? I left that store feeling infuriated and swore I would never buy there again. I'd never waste another minute of my time in that place. It would have been easier to steal the merchandise than it would have been to buy the merchandise. When I got back home, I opened the mail and what did I find? A slick invitation from that same department store inviting me to come down and shop their big sale!

Service is always senior to selling, always. One of the best people I know who is an example of high levels of service is my friend, Gavin Potter. While I consider Gavin a friend he sells me constantly on contributing money for projects for which he raises money. I consider him a friend and not a salesperson because of the extraordinary amount of service he gives me. He is an incredible salesperson, but above that, he's dedicated to high levels of service and thoroughly convinced of his cause. His commitment to his purpose alone and his dedication to high levels of service is what makes him great. One without the other results in mediocrity! Gavin has both barrels loaded: service and purpose. I guarantee you that if Gavin were to run his statistics he would find that his sales rise with every service-oriented action he performs. He knows that service is senior to the sale and this is why he is in a league of his own as a salesperson.

If you incorporate these simple truths about giving and providing stellar service, I assure you that you'll become a master of your trade. You'll experience a confidence that you cannot put any value on and that is worth more than money itself. You'll be able to name your price, go where you want, work with whom you choose, sell whatever products you choose to sell and provide for yourself and your family in ways that most people only dream of! You'll also experience a lifestyle that very few people actually have-- one free of stress, worry and problems. So give, give, give of yourself fully and provide unparalleled levels of service!

Chapter Eleven Questions:

In your own words what does the author mean when he writes, "Selling is about giving not getting, servicing not selling?"

What are four things you could give away other than the lowest price, products or services:

1)

2)

3)

4)

Give actual examples of how you give something without it costing you anything:

1)

2)

3)

4)

What does the author mean when he says love the one you are with?

What things would you have to improve immediately about yourself to be rated as a Ritz Carlton?

1)

2)

3)

4)

What is the only way to higher prices and less competition?

Any questions? Call 800-368-5771

HARD SELL

The Hard Sell

It has been said that you have to ask someone five times before you get a yes. I do not know if that is true or not, but I do know that most people will not buy without someone asking them to and people will never say yes to someone who quit asking. It has been my experience that the moment you quit asking, the deal is dead.

It's also been my experience that most people will not just give you the money without you asking and persisting and being willing to "hard sell." I'm not talking about pressuring the buyer. I'm talking about being willing to get to that hard place in the close where everyone gets a little bit uncomfortable. The salesperson must be willing to stay in the deal and persist through to the close because they believe deep down inside that the product or service is right for the buyer. The salesperson must be willing to persist even when it gets hard, difficult or uncomfortable and that is what is meant by "hard sell."

A buyer once told me, "Grant, you're pressuring me." To that I explained, "Sir, you're confusing my belief and passion in knowing this is the right product for you and your company with pressure. Please don't misinterpret my enthusiasm for pressure, now lets do this."

When you hit "hard sell" status you've become so convinced that your company or product is the only answer and any other choice would be a disservice. At the place of "hard sell" you're certain that your service is superior to anyone anywhere and ultimately the only right choice your customer can make and you insist on it because of this belief! Because you believe this so deeply you're willing to stay in the deal even when it gets uncomfortable and people are squirming and making excuses and becoming difficult.

One of the best salespeople I've ever met is a woman named Charmaigne. She's a full-time fundraiser and a dedicated master of her trade. Charmaigne isn't selling a tangible product; rather, she's raising money for charity to help people around the world. She called me up one night and asked for an appointment. I agreed, but made it clear that I wouldn't be making any more contributions as I'd already fulfilled my charitable donations for the year. "Yes, no problem," she said. "I just want to come over to see you and catch up." She came over and we talked for a while and then she asked me to think about donating more. I adamantly told her, "No! Absolutely not! No way! I already told you that I'd donated all that I'm donating for the year. I am done Charmaigne!" Unshaken by my outburst, she looked at me with a smile and said, "Now Grant, the only reason you're acting like this is, you know you haven't done enough." I couldn't believe her audacity to take everything I'd just said and handle me! Once the initial shock wore off, I started laughing and did what all people do when they're sold, I gave more. Charmaigne is dedicated to her cause, which is what makes her a master fundraiser. She could have been "polite" and left when I started hollering at her and things got uncomfortable. But she didn't. She stayed and she got the close. The willingness to stay and persist even when the prospect becomes noisy is what separates the professional, consistent closer from the amateur who randomly closes deals.

If you don't truly believe that your product will somehow bring the buyer more enjoyment, benefit or security greater than the numbers they have in the bank, then you'll never be a great salesperson and you'll never fully understand the concept of "hard sell." If you really believe and learn how to close you'll know someday what it means to be hard sell. This is an art form!

The Formula for Hard Sell

There are only two things that can get you to the point of being a true professional hard sell closer:

1. You must have the belief that what you're offering is the right thing for the prospect.

2. You have to be trained to stay in the close *no matter what happens*. You'll need to be armed with an arsenal of ways to handle stalls, emotional reactions and objections. My closing program is vital for arming you up with the technology to master the hard sell. Go to www.grantcardone. com or call 800-368-5771.

Closing is Like a Recipe

There is no way around the fact that you have to know what to say and it has to sound natural. Does this mean you need to become rote in your responses and have some formulated way to handle a specific objection? Absolutely! It's like a recipe. It takes certain ingredients combined together in a certain order and put into the oven at a certain temperature for a certain amount of time. Do it exactly per the recipe and you get what you anticipated, change one thing and you will not. The more you practice handling objections, the more natural you'll sound. It is like the grandmother who makes fudge without even looking at the recipe. She has done it so many times over the years that she does not need to read over the list of ingredients anymore. She just knows what to do and the fudge comes out perfect every time. It is the same thing with handling objections and closing deals. There is nothing wrong with learning what you're going to say and how you'll handle certain situations.

If you were giving a press conference to the world, you'd drill and practice what you were going to say. You'd consider how your address would be perceived and the effect that it might create before you'd go out in front of the world with it. You'll have to do the same thing to prepare yourself to become a professional "hard sell" closer.

You need to practice handling objections and stalls so that you can persist intelligently through resistance. I practiced this daily for years. Every morning I'd team up with another salesperson and we'd practice every possible situation we could possibly encounter that day. This turned me into a lethal individual at closing deals. If you can't close, you lose.

I've done this in many different industries only to find out that all objections are similar and the closing techniques cross over from one industry to the next. If you can't persist with closes due to the fact that you run out of material then you'll never reach the level of being hard sell! If you don't learn how to hard sell you will not make it to be one of the greats!

I suggested to you earlier to work out how you're going to handle situations. I don't want you looking shocked or surprised or having to run off somewhere to figure out what to do. I don't want you going home to think about what you could have done differently — leave that for the amateurs. For you to be a professional and to get professional results, you have to know what you'll do and say in every situation.

Video yourself and perfect your techniques. I recorded myself everyday and watched my gestures, hand motions, even my emotional responses. Throughout the day I'd write down all of the objections I heard and the next day I'd team up with another associate and we'd practice handling them until I was satisfied. Drilling and practice builds confidence. You're already doing this now whether you know it or not but you are doing it to build bad habits, not good ones.

Standing is for Losing, Sitting is for Closing

I've watched salespeople enter negotiations standing up which is a common error. They stand there talking about their prices, payment plans,

Any questions? Call 800-368-5771

programs, guarantees and benefits and in so doing are only talking and not showing. No wonder they aren't closing! They're talking too much and not using anything to establish their credibility. Remember your buyer will believe what he sees not what he hears! Talking and telling isn't closing and won't even remotely get a salesperson a shot at the close!

You'll almost never close a deal if you're standing up. Sit your client down and show them what you can do for them and support it with facts they can see and substantiate. Standing up is for walking; sitting down is for closing. So sit your customer down and get your buyer in a position to be closed. *"Sit right here sir and let me SHOW you the facts about the product."* Don't pitch it, show it. When you're making a proposal, sit the buyer down and write down the facts and figures. Telling him verbally is a waste of time and effort and almost never results in a close. So sit the buyer down and show him what you've got and be prepared to hard sell in order to close the deal.

Chapter Twelve Questions:

How is "hard sell" different from pressuring someone?

What is a great way to handle someone that suggests you are pressuring them?

What are the two things you have to become convinced about in order to reach hard sell status?

1)

2)

What is the Formula for Hard Sell?

1)

2)

What are the 3 suggestions the author makes in order for you to learn how to hard sell?

1)

2)

3)

CHAPTER THIRTEEN

MASSIVE
ACTION

Take Massive Action

Most people incorrectly estimate the amount of effort it takes to get the results they want. When it comes to taking action, never think in terms of balance, always think in terms of massive amounts of action. Assume in the case of action that more is better and less is nothing. Whatever you think you need to do to get the job done, increase the amount far greater than you think is necessary and you'll get results beyond your wildest expectations.

Never let the psychiatrist types convince you with their psychobabble, mumbo-jumbo that you need "balance" in your life or that you should "stop pushing yourself" and "live in the moment." This advice is promulgated by those who apparently want you to have a mediocre life and they have no evidence to substantiate this advice as valuable. The more I work and accomplish, the better I feel. The less I do, the more tired I feel. When it comes to getting big results and becoming wildly successful you have to take action in that direction in massive quantities. There's no way around it.

I love action and the more the better! I love getting things done and I bet you do too! I love the satisfaction of accomplishing a task. I'm happiest when I'm producing and creating. I love working in my yard more than I like lying on my sofa.

If you want to get anyplace in life, you've got to take action. If you want to take a trip, you've got to fill the tank with fuel and then accelerate the car down the highway. If you want to build a house you've got to pound nails and pour concrete. If you want to win the lottery, you've got to buy a ticket! To get results you have to take action! The amount of success you have is limited by the amount of action you take. Stay away from the people who tell you to stop working so hard and suggest you should relax and take it easy. You can take it easy once you make it. For now, take action and take it in massive quantities.

I took massive action in my life and have done so until it became a way of life, a discipline. Am I a maniac? I certainly don't think so, and I can tell you that I'm living a life that no one in my entire heritage has ever experienced. Do you think a man gets elected President of the United States without taking massive action to ensure he gets elected? Do you think Tiger Woods didn't take massive action to become the greatest golfer in the world? Mr. Woods out-practices everyone in his field and because of this dedication to massive action, he's reached levels that others never dreamed of! To become President in your field, you will have to be out of balance, totally focused and dedicated, following up with tremendous amounts of actions.

The 4 Degrees of Action

You can never take enough action in life, you can only take too little. Too much action will never get you into trouble. In fact, taking action is the way to get *out of trouble*. The only time that action will cause you trouble is when there isn't any or when there's not enough of it.

It's been said that there are three degrees of action in life.

1) The right action

2) The wrong action

3) No action (which will always result in nothing).

And in my world there's a fourth action.

4) Massive action! That's the one I live by!

The fourth action, *Massive Action*, is by far the most successful tool I've had in my life and has resulted in more success for me than any other single thing I've done. When someone asks me what one thing made the most difference in my life, this is it -- Massive Action. Even when I had no clue what I was doing, I went ahead and took massive action. If I wanted to get a loan on a piece of property, I always went to three or four lenders. When I bought a piece of property, I made bids on more than one property. When I throw a party, I invite lots of people and then repeat the invitations. When I'm done with invites I get on the phone and I keep calling until I'm guaranteed a great party. I don't like small parties. I like them big and noisy with lots of people. I'd rather have too many than too few. One time I had a party at my home and went through 2500 plastic cups! Now that's the sign of a real party! I didn't even know half of the people that were there. You've heard the saying, go big or go home? I say go massive, not passive!

Massive Action = New Problems

I watch salespeople make a few phone calls, send out a few pieces of mail and then stop to take a coffee break and gossip about the latest news in the local paper. Then they sit down and chatter about how business is slow and how the phone and prospecting doesn't get them results.

If you worked the phone the way I do, you'd know that the phone does <u>not</u> work, it's the person on the phone who's working. I never sit down to make one phone call, never! When I sit down to use the phone I do it with enough tenacity and massive amounts of quantity that I'm guaranteed to get something in return from my actions!

If it's appointments you want, take massive action until your concern is no longer whether or not you'll get enough appointments, but how you can possibly handle all of the appointments you have. The right amount of massive action should result in new problems.

One of my goals in my seminar business is to sell out the locations to the point where there aren't enough chairs to seat the attendees. This always worries my sales guys because they don't want the customers to get upset after paying $800 for a ticket and not having a chair. That's a new and good problem! One of my salespeople protested that this wasn't fair to the audience. I said, "Bring it on ding dong! You fill the place up to a point where people don't have a place to sit and I'll handle the fallout." Never worry about the wrong things because you won't ever get what you want! Doing too much will never fail you, doing too little always will.

When it comes to action, go big, go bold and then go more. This is the *one thing* that will guarantee results. Don't deal in small numbers and small actions. Deal in large numbers and massive volumes of action. Go massive, not passive.

When I was a young salesperson I was rough around the edges and my wife says that I still am. But I never let that stop me from taking action. When you're not perfect and polished, the only way to compensate is by taking lots of action. You'll find that when you get enough volume going you don't have to be perfect! You'll never become polished at this career if you've only got a handful of opportunities. The more action you take, the more business you'll have and the better you'll get at your job.

If you're <u>unlucky</u> enough to be one of those polished and professional types you'll still need to take massive action in order to get to the higher levels of production. I say "unlucky" because I've met many veteran salespeople who have been around for years and are very professional and know their business. But they have this air about them that they're superior to others and don't have to keep learning and changing and taking action. Wake up! It takes massive action, not polish to get what you want in life! No one will pay you for what you know. They'll pay you for what you do!

Production Yields Happiness

Most people don't get enough in life only because they never do enough in life! Production makes people feel good. It almost doesn't matter what you're producing just so long as you're doing and producing something constructive. Decide to produce something and produce it in massive quantities and you will win in life! Production results in happiness. This is a basic truth found in every religious, economic and ethnic group on this planet. Man feels better when he's producing, and the more production he generates, the better he will feel. Money may not make one happy, but production will. "Man was born to work hard (Dr. Michael Debakey)."

In sales, massive action is the one single thing that will guarantee you increased success more than any other! If you want to guarantee X, take massive amounts of action that will achieve X in abundance. Your new problem will no longer be how to achieve an abundance of X, rather, how to manage the abundance of X.

Massive Action = New Problems. It is at this point that you know you are doing enough, short of a new problem that you haven't taken enough action!

Throw a pebble in a pond and it creates a ripple.

Pound the pond with mortar round after mortar round and then follow up with more mortar rounds and you'll create a massive lake and everyone around will come to see what you are doing!

By taking enough massive action, something will be changed, something will be created and results will be attained! In the sales arena, massive action is like the stairway to heaven where the sales gods will praise you with trophies, trips, rewards and the guarantee of new levels of income! Your fellow salespeople, however, may praise you only with criticism, tell you that you're working too hard and give you free advice like, "Slow down—smell the roses." Disregard them and consider their suppressive comments as a sign that you are on the right track and continue to add wood to your fire. All fire requires you to continue to add wood and success in sales requires more action.

Anyone who tells you that you're working too hard is not working hard enough. Unfortunately, such people have given up their hopes of having an extraordinary life. Such people are mediocre at best and have forgotten about the dreams they used to have. Take massive actions until you get new problems at which point, you will get new levels of sales results. Don't quit until you get new problems like taxes, cars, homes and where to go on vacation.

Any questions? Call 800-368-5771

The 10X Rule

If you want one thing, take massive action equal to at least *ten times* what you think it will take to ensure you attain that one thing. If you do this you won't have to hope, wish, cross your fingers or pray because what you want *and far more* will come to you when the right amount of action is created!

A salesperson once told me about the bad luck he'd been experiencing. His appointment cancelled, a buyer backed out, another customer had to change his order, and so on. I told him that his problem wasn't bad luck or misfortune, but that he didn't have enough in his pipeline. I suggested that if he took ten times more action that he had been, he'd have no attention on these so-called misfortunes and would have actually welcomed someone canceling out as it would have been a relief to his situation rather than misfortune.

If you take enough action and are getting results then it's no big deal when an appointment cancels or a buyer backs out. In fact, you'll welcome the occasional cancellation so you can get to everyone on your line up. But if you're only taking small amounts of action every time you lose a deal all of your attention goes on the so called misfortune and the loss because you don't have anything to replace it with. You've put too much attention on too little. Put your attention on massive to ensure you don't become passive.

Act Like a Madman

An associate of mine watched me call a client fifteen times in three days without the client ever returning my call. Is this too much? I don't think so. When I want to get something done, I keep taking action until I get what I want. Never be reasonable when it comes to taking action, just take more action. Be almost insane with how much action you take to get the job done.

A farmer should plant far more than he can possibly eat so if a drought or famine occurs he can still take care of his family and his neighbors. A realtor who wants listings should call hundreds of people to get just one and will probably end up with many. If you want appointments, call every friend you have, every past client and stop people on the streets if that is what it takes. Be mad in how much action you take until it becomes a habit, a way of life and normal for you. Once you are greatly successful, people will talk about how successful they always knew you would be, rather than how crazy you were. In no time you'll be overflowing with appointments, sales and success.

Act like a madman when it comes to action and get completely unreasonable about what you think it will take to get the job done. Be without sanity or logic or reason when it comes to taking massive amounts of action and you'll reach heights that others never dreamed possible. Massive actions equals first new problems, then will equal massive sales.

Chapter Thirteen Questions:

What is the one thing the author states that most people incorrectly estimate in order to get the results they want?

Write down a time when you underestimated the amount of effort that was required in order to reach a goal and how much did you underestimate the effort?

What are the Four Degrees of Action?

1)

2)

3)

4)

What will one immediately experience from taking massive action?

The author says that most people never get enough in life because... (finish the statement)

What is the 10x Rule?

Any questions? Call 800-368-5771

THE POWER BASE

Work Your Power Base

Salespeople tend to put their attention on selling to people that they don't know and ignoring the people they do know. Entire companies advertise to people they don't know, haven't sold and to people who are not even interested in their products. Salespeople wait for people they don't know and even call people they don't know, while completely ignoring their known lines of influence. This is an absolute violation of creating power and one of the most violated basics that salespeople overlook in their careers.

Everyone has a base of power in their life where things are familiar and known. Typically, it starts with one's family and friends. Most everyone has a place where there's some element of understanding, comprehension, safety, security and strength. The easiest sale you'll ever make in your life is to those people that already know you, trust you and want to help you. Everyone has a power base or a fan club. Don't ignore it, work it, use it and mine it like gold.

Your power base is made up of the people that will be happy to hear from you and want to know what you're up to. One of the fastest ways to not get into power in your career is to abandon those that love you, care for you and have some interest in your life. Therefore, no one has to start from scratch. Everyone knows someone.

I had a customer who had bought many products from me and we became personal friends. I called him up one day and I told him, "get over here right now, I have to show you something." He asked me what I was up to and I repeated, "just get over here as soon as you can." Not long after he showed up at my office, I pulled out the buyer's order and told him to sign it. He asked, "sign it? But I don't even know what I'm buying." I assured him, "don't worry about it. I'd never mislead you and I guarantee that you're going to want this." He signed the order, I presented him with his product and he fell in love with it! It was that simple. I sold him something he wasn't in the market for, didn't know he needed and it was one of the easiest sales of my life. You can do things like this with your powerbase. Think of yourself of the center of the base and the closer to the center of the base the individual is, the easier the sale.

How to Build Your Powerbase

The first thing you need to do is make a list of your powerbase. You powerbase includes, but is not limited to, friends, family members, associates at past jobs, past employers, current and former clients, members of clubs, neighbors, organizations you belong to, members of your church, and believe it or not, even people that didn't like you in high school.

Who are they, where are they, how do you contact them and what should you say? What you say to them is the easiest part. Just tell them what you're doing. First make your list and then make contact! Let them know what you're up to and find out when you can meet with them to catch up. The purpose of the meeting is not to sell them because that will happen naturally. The purpose is to get in contact with them and to work and restore your powerbase.

If you've come up with a list of ten people, automatically consider that number to be at least one hundred. Each of the people you know will have at least ten people in their powerbase who can benefit from what you're selling or the service that you're offering. If you don't believe that this is true, then I suggest you go back to the earlier chapter in this book and resell yourself on what you're doing.

You can contact these people by phone, in person, by mail or by email. The best way is to meet face to face if possible, so go drop in or call and set up a time to have lunch. Don't worry if you've completely neglected these people for years. Forget the past and go catch up with them and create your future! Take interest in your contacts and mine your powerbase. Find out about them, what they're doing, their work, the family and everything that's going on. Restore the relationships. When it comes around to you, let them know what you're doing and how much you love it. You can breech the subject that you'd love to show them your product, but at this point your intention is to simply restore, rebuild and mine your powerbase.

Impose on Them or Help Them?

People want to help people that they know. Put away any reservations that you have and contact them. Get rid of that silly consideration about not wanting to impose on the relationship. That's ridiculous. What are friends and family for if you can't impose on that relationship so that you can help them! Someone is going to sell them, why not you? The reality is they want to help you as well. If you love your product and fully believe in it, then love your powerbase enough to let them know what you've got. Rely on the earlier rule about taking massive action and use it on your powerbase. Contact enough people in your powerbase and someone will tell you that they need your product or service. And if you have a problem imposing, you are really having a problem on being sold and need to get that back again.

From there you can expand your list.

Let's say I sell clothes and I have ten friends, each of whom has a use for the kind of clothing I am selling. Each of those people has an average of 2.2 more people in their household. That is twenty-two people expanded from ten.

Let those first twenty-two people know what you do, what you sell, where you are and how they can contact you. Get their addresses and put them on a mailing list. Collect their birthdays, or if you want just send out random birthday cards. No birthday card is better responded to than one that's been sent out on the wrong day. Everyone will call you informing you that you have the wrong date for their birthday at which point you'll say, "I know that, but I didn't know what your actual birthday was, and thought I would take a chance at being right!" I guarantee you they'll call. You have to get creative about contacting people. A little imagination combined with massive action goes a long way and don't ever worry about making a mistake. The only mistake you can make is by making no contact.

Get these twenty-two people to help you meet the people they know so you can start working that list. Work the powerbase from the inside out and watch how big it gets.

When you're making your powerbase list you're going to be shocked at all of the people you've forgotten. Don't worry about it, just make contact! They'll be glad to hear from you and want to help you.

I once contacted a guy from high school that I used to get into fights with and was adversaries with as a teenager. I called him up and told him that even though twenty years had passed I still thought about him often and had laughed at how we'd been enemies. Not long after that he came into my office and bought my product from me. Speaking from experience, I can tell you that it's easier to sell a past enemy that it is someone you've never met! Don't deny your powerbase. Work it!

If you don't help your powerbase, a guy like me will. All of us have had the experience of running into an old friend who owns a product that we represent, but who had bought it from a competitor. The competition had worked the prospect and you lost a sale because you simply failed to contact your powerbase.

The worst part about making a sale is that you just lost your best prospect and now need to replace him! This new customer now becomes part of your power base. Ask any salesperson anywhere, "would you rather sell someone that you've never met or someone that you've sold to before?" If you were to poll a million salespeople with that question, all would agree that they want to sell to someone they've already sold. Why? Because they have the experience of winning with that customer, it is easier to sell them again. The relationship is there, trust is there and an experience is there. This is your powerbase now getting bigger. Add this to the enlarging circle that is emanating from you and stay in contact with these people.

Capitalize on the Easy Sale

Existing customers are the easiest sale there is to make and I always prefer them over a brand new prospect. I know what turns them on, I have a relationship, I have their trust, they know me, the company and the products I represent! Even when an existing customer has a complaint or a problem, there's still a great opportunity to turn the complaint or problem into another sale.

I have a policy in my office that all complaints are to be immediately brought to me. Why would I want to deal with complaints? Because I know that complaints are one of the most overlooked opportunities for additional sales. Problems are opportunities! Solve the problem and you gain an even better customer.

Another reason that former customers are easier to sell is because it's easier for them to make a decision with someone they've done business with before. People are creatures of habit. When I do a sales seminar, ninety-nine percent of the people choose to sit next to someone that they know. Why? People find comfort in familiarity.

Creating Power!

Most salespeople don't capitalize on this enough. I like doing business with people that I know. I like it that you already know what I like, what I want and how to talk to me. I like it that you already know what my expectations are and how I want to be serviced. I like it that we have an experience that we survived together. But I wonder if the salesperson feels the same way because he rarely calls me after he sells me.

Do you not think I'll buy another suit, another computer, another cell phone, television, house, appliance, car, another piece of property or make another investment? Do you think I'm done after I played with you once? Do you think I ran out of money or that this was the last time any human being would close me on a similar product? Do you think that you captured the entire amount of my credit limit? Always remember, you won't be the person that sells the customer for the last time. The question is, will you sell him the next time? I can assure you that if you don't stay in touch with your powerbase including your previous customers, you'll never attain power in your business. Never neglect your former customers!

If you want to guarantee certainty in your sales production and assure yourself a long and happy career in selling, stay in touch with the people in your powerbase. Love them, call them, wine and dine them, send them presents and continue to show interest in them.

I bought my first real estate investment from a friend. He'd been told by his mentor after months of working with me that I would never buy anything from him and that he was wasting his time with me. I bought forty-eight units and the following month bought another thirty-eight units. So much for the mentor with the great advice. But the story doesn't stop there. This guy became my partner and quit the firm he was working for to manage the property that I had bought from him. He thought I was done after these first two purchases and quit aggressively looking to buy more! I'd call him stating that I was looking for more deals and he was pessimistic of the prices and my probable ability to purchase more. Another, long-term friend of mine, Dale, was in my office after I'd hung up with my new partner in frustration. Dale asked if he could find me deals would I give him the same deal as my other partner. I told him yes and shortly there after bought another 400 units over the next two years and then bought another 1500 units after that.

My first partner is a great guy and did very well for himself, but he violated his power base! My old friend, Dale made millions off the deal by staying close to his powerbase and working it! By the way, Dale had no experience in real estate and the first guy did. He was flat broke at the time we hooked up and he was fifty-two-years-old with less than sixty dollars to his name. That's a true story and today he's a multimillionaire. Dale never should have gotten the chance to become my partner, but he did because the first partner violated his power base. Dale saw the opportunity of his own powerbase and he worked it. The moral of the story is to stay in touch with the people in your powerbase.

Keep as much attention on the people you just sold as you do the people that you want to sell next. And build power from your powerbase!

Chapter Fourteen Questions:

What does the author suggest is one of the most violated basics people overlook when trying to sell their ideas or products?

Make a list of ten people in your power base?

1)   6)

2)   7)

3)   8)

4)   9)

5)   10)

What is the worst part of making a sale?

What is one of the most overlooked opportunities for additional sales?

What are the five reasons the author suggests that an existing or past customer is an easier sale than someone you don't know?

1)

2)

3)

4)

5)

Any questions? Call 800-368-5771

TIME

How Much Time Do You Have?

The most powerful man in the world has 24 hours in a day to get what he needs done. The richest man in the world has 3600 minutes in a day to earn his money. The most educated man in the world has 168 hours a week to learn. The greatest athlete in the worlds has 365 days in a year to train. How much time do you have?

When people tell me that they don't have enough time to get what they need done, I don't believe it. I recently read that the average person in this country watches three hours of television a day which translates into 67,500 minutes. Do you realize how many phone calls you could make in a year with that much time? If every call only lasted three minutes you could make an extra

22,500 phone calls a year. That would be 1875 calls a month or 75 calls a day! If you only did a portion of that you would reach the top half of the top one-percent of all the salespeople in your industry.

It's actually a LIE when you tell yourself that you don't have enough time! The fact is, you have the same amount of time as everyone else and just aren't using it efficiently. We all have the same twenty-four hour days amounting to 8,760 hours a year. If you don't know how much time is available, I assure you that you haven't decided how to use it. If you agree that time is money, then your time should be inventoried and protected like you would anything that is valuable.

I had to travel to Las Vegas recently for a speaking engagement. As my driver dropped me off at the airport he asked when I'd be coming home so he could arrange to pick me up. I told him I'd be arriving back the following day before noon. He then suggested, "Why don't you enjoy yourself and spend an extra night and come back the following morning?" I told him, "Rather than wasting time in Vegas and make them richer, I'll come home and get back to work and maybe make myself richer. Who knows? Maybe by being home and being in the office I'll close the biggest deal of my life." "Ahh," he said, "That's why you're where you are and I'm driving you." Exactly! And that's how you will get where you want to go – by maximizing every minute of every day. Anyone can be where they are now. The question is, can you get to the next place? Only by using time wisely.

Use Every Moment to Sell

I'd been selling for a couple of years and this man named Ray had taken me under his wing because he saw some promise in me. He pulled me aside one day and asked, "Grant, why do you go to lunch with your fellow salesperson Gene so often?" I was perplexed by the question because it seemed perfectly natural that I'd go to lunch with my friend and co-worker. When I wasn't able to answer, Ray looked at me and said, "Grant, Gene will never buy anything from you, never!"

Wow! What he said fell on me like a truckload of gold bricks and it really got me to confront how much time, energy and money I'd wasted by going to lunch with Gene. As I thought about it, I realized I'd been wasting one hour every day, six times a week for fifty two weeks of the year. I'd spent 312 hours of my time with no opportunity whatsoever at making a sale! I never went to lunch with Gene again after that, and my sales began to pick up. I made it a firm policy that if I wasn't eating with clients or potential clients, I'd eat lunch in my office while I called clients.

How Much Time Are You Wasting?

Starting today, I want you to take a look at how much time you waste in a day. Every time you find yourself doing something that is not productive, make note of it. Smoking, taking coffee breaks, standing in line, calling friends or family, gossiping, standing around the water cooler, discussing the game, going to bars, doodling, daydreaming, avoiding work, etc. Write it down and become aware of all the things you're doing that don't add up to moving your team and your company down the field. What if you only had one hour to win the game? You can't take breaks when you've got to work the ball down the field. You only have three, one-minute time outs and you're on the clock. When the buzzer rings, the game is over!

He who makes the most of his time will accomplish the most. Make the decision now that you're controlling time – that time is no longer controlling you. Change your mind about time and decide that you have plenty of it. Become a master of the clock, not a slave to it.

The Lunch Opportunity

A partner and I were at a lunch meeting with a group of potential clients. The group seated my partner and me together, so I requested that we be seated at different tables. Why? Because I can't sell my partner and there is no opportunity in sitting next to him! The goal was to be with as many of these clients as possible, not to be with each other. I sat at one table and he sat at another, thus doubling our exposure.

I learned this valuable lesson back when I was a sales person wasting lunches with my co-worker Gene. Today I won't go to lunch with a fellow salesperson, a manager or even the boss. I need to spend time with customers. Going to lunch with your boss will not get you job security, but selling more products will. My rule is if they work with me, they won't buy from me and that excludes them from spending lunch with me. You need to work your sales career the way a politician works his campaign. He doesn't keep talking to the people that are already going to vote for him. He goes and talks to the people who haven't yet decided.

Today I invest my lunchtime, breakfast and dinners with buyers, prospects and even long shots. These lunch dates would include anyone that might someday buy from me. Even when I'm not taking a customer to lunch I'll frequent places where I've got a shot at being seen, where people go or where I might just luck out and run into someone who will buy from me.

People that go out for lunch are typically qualified buyers. They're people who are working: bankers, insurance people, salespeople, entrepreneurs, etc. These are the buyers of your products. Go out and be with them, be seen by them and get to know them. Find a restaurant where qualified people go out to eat and show up there everyday until you get to know the scene. Visit that one place and become known there before moving on to other locations. Get to know the owner and the waitresses until they know you by your first name. Then you'll get to know the patrons. Go to the places where potential customers congregate at lunch and be seen by them. Personally, I like to go to the pricier restaurants because they attract the better quality customers. Aristotle Onasis, the great shipping magnate, always made a point to go to the most expensive restaurants throughout his travels when he was a young man. Not because he could afford it, but because the people there had money and he wanted to be around opportunity and success!

I once made a sale to an insurance agent and offered to buy him lunch as a sign of my appreciation. I met him at his office where we loaded up his wife and daughter and went off to his favorite place. At the time I was thinking small and was worried about how much the bill was going to be. Within five minutes of sitting down, he'd already introduced me to a friend of his at another table. My client's intro was, "Vic, this is the kid I was telling you about," at which time Vic pulls out a card and says, "I want one just like he got. Can you have it at my office today?"

Any questions? Call 800-368-5771

Lunch Out = Sales Up!

That brown bag lunch you made to save yourself ten dollars will cost you hundreds of thousands of dollars in lost sales. Go out, be seen, mix it up and put yourself in the game. Use your lunchtime to meet clients and don't waste this opportunity hanging out with friends and other employees. You can't save your way to being a millionaire, but you can certainly sell your way there! Quit trying to save money and start doing whatever it takes to be seen, to get noticed and to make sales!

My wife is an actress here in Hollywood, and I asked her where the best place is for people in her business to be seen. She told me that the place to be seen is at the Ivy. Well guess where we go to lunch now? People remember who they see and forget who they don't see. Some people even take it as a "sign" when they see you that they should do something with you.

Lunch is about business and opportunity. It's not about food, friends and family. Lunch is an occasion to create contacts and show appreciation for past customers! Utilize it and work this one-hour goldmine. Make the most of every day by knocking out the wasted time and cleverly schedule the use of your valuable time! Some people might wonder, isn't there any time to just relax and take it easy? Sure there is, but that comes later when you've reached your goals and made your dreams come true.

If you aren't where you want to be in life, you've got to work every angle, every minute and snatch up every opportunity. You owe it to yourself, your family and your future! Make every moment count.

Chapter Fifteen Questions:

How much time do you have. Don't look.

Write down all activities that you consider to be a waste of time for you and how much time you think you waste in that activity a week:

1)

2)

3)

4)

5)

6)

Multiply each of the above by 52 and then by 20 to calculate the cost of that activity to you every year in time and money:

1)

2)

3)

4)

5)

6)

Write down the two activities that make you the most money and how much time you spend on this each week:

1)

2)

ATTITUDE

A Great Attitude is Worth More Than a Great Product

People will pay more for an agreeable, positive and enjoyable experience than they will for a great product. Who doesn't want to feel good? Who doesn't want to be acknowledged for being right? Who doesn't want to be smiled at and agreed with? Show me a person that doesn't want to feel good and I'll show you someone that you don't want to bother selling! Man wants to feel good. Man is moved by positive and confident people, more than he is moved by great products. There will always be a market for products that make him feel good, but a person who can *make* someone feel good can sell almost anything! The individual that combines a great attitude with a great product becomes unstoppable!

A positive attitude is a thousand times more important than the product itself. Just observe how people on this planet spend their money. A person will spend a small amount of his income on the necessities of life and blow his entire paycheck on entertainment. Why? Because he wants to feel good! Why does Jay Leno make more money than all of the school teachers in Los Angeles combined? Because he makes people laugh and feel good.

It's easy for a buyer to say no to a product or a company, but it's extremely difficult to say no to a positive experience with another human being. When something makes you feel good you want more of it whether it makes sense or not. This is why people do things that aren't good for them because for a moment or two, it made them feel good. People will spend money on things that make them feel good before they'll spend money on things they need. This explains the poverty and debt levels we see today!

One time I saw a beautiful jacket on display in a shop window and was so intrigued by it that I went inside to have a closer look. I asked the clerk the price, which she told me as she helped me slip on the jacket. Admiring my reflection in the mirror, I protested that the price was insane and added that I didn't even need the thing! With a warm, understanding and beautiful smile she said, "No one buys a jacket like this because they need it. They buy it because it's beautiful and it makes them feel good." Melting in the truth of her statement, I asked her, "Do you take AMEX?"

With all the chaos and bad news that the media disseminates daily, it's refreshing to meet a solution-oriented, positive person. You know the kind of person I'm talking about. The kind of person who's always smiling as they say, "Yes sir, I'll get it done for you, I'd be happy to do that!" I want to be taken care of by positive people. I don't want to just be sold. I want people around me who are positive, helpful, smiling and motivated. That's what all people want.

I have a personal assistant named Jen. When I hired her she had no experience with the type of businesses I own and had never worked in the kind of environment we have. I didn't hire Jen because of her abilities and experience, but because of her positive attitude. Jen is an upbeat "can do," "get it done" with-a-smile-on-her-face kind of a person. It doesn't mean that Jen doesn't make mistakes, she does. But because of her attitude, the mistakes are acceptable. I never get mad at her no matter what she does because she's so service oriented, so positive, so "Yes sir, I'd be happy to do that for you." Is Jen selling? Absolutely! Every day whether she knows it or not.

Never let anyone convince you that people won't pay more for a great attitude and great service. The ability to be positive at all times, whether you're winning or losing is the one thing that will ensure you're a winner in the end. Attitude is senior to it all! I love positive people and find them irresistible. When you are positive, people will find you irresistible.

Treat 'em Like Millionaires

My wife and I often go to a place called The Grove for dinner and a movie. We valet park the car there and this bleached blonde, spiky-haired guy always greets us, opens the car door and smiles like he's glad to see us. "Good to see you again, boss," he says. "Leave it with me. I'll see you in a couple of hours and your car will be right up front." He gets a twenty dollar tip from me every time even though I could have parked the car myself for two dollars. The other valet guy who works there greets us like we're a nuisance, doesn't smile, appears to hate his job and parks the car in the same spot that the spiky-haired guy does. Due to his poor attitude, I give him five dollars and that's only because the guy parked my car for me. I'm sure he then goes home and tells his girlfriend how cheap all the people are that valet their big cars and that his spiky-haired partner is just luckier than he is.

It ain't the luck of the spiky-haired guy, I assure you and it is definitely not that I'm a poor tipper. It's the attitude that makes the difference. The reality is, people with good attitudes are luckier than people with bad attitudes! There is no treasure greater than a great attitude and no way to get real treasures without having a great attitude!

A customer wanted to buy a truck from me one time and he, like many car buyers didn't want the dealership to make any money off the deal. He thought it was fair that he only pay invoice for the truck. None of this makes any sense, of course, because if the company sells their products for invoice then they won't be able to stay in business to service the customer.

But because I know that attitude is more important than the product or the price and because I trusted that the customer would pay for my positive, can-do attitude, I told him, "No problem whatever you want, it's yours my friend. I just appreciate having the opportunity to do business with you." He was shocked at my response and the smile I had on my face because I hadn't let him get beneath my skin. I spent the next hour or so with him showing him the truck, getting to know him, laughing with him, and being a positive influence on him. I treated the customer as if he were about to give me a million dollars. I put aside the fact that he didn't want to pay above invoice for the product and pushed everything in the direction of a great attitude!

At the close, I showed him the documented invoice price on the truck, state taxes of $4000 and added an additional $2000 for me to take care of him for the next four years. He looked at me and said, "I know I can buy this down the street without paying the extra two thousand." With a smile I responded, "You're probably right, but you won't get me down the street." He laughed and said, "I don't know why I'm doing this, but let's do it," and he wrote the check.

Remember that a product can be shopped, but a great attitude cannot. A price can be beat, but a great attitude is priceless. There's nothing more valuable to anyone than a positive person.

People will always act according to your attitude. If it's negative expect a negative response. When it's positive you can expect a positive response. If I scream and threaten another person you can expect them to flee or fight. Neither response is good for a salesperson. But if I'm positive and agreeable I can expect the buyer's response to be the same if I'm contagious enough! When you have the ability to change another's attitude in a positive way and make them feel better than they did before meeting you, you'll no longer need to rely on your product being superior!

How you act toward others will be how they'll act toward you. Your attitude precedes everything that happens to you in life. If you think about car wrecks, you'll have car wrecks. If you hang around with negative people, you'll start to get negative. Hang around people with problems and you'll attract problems.

A Product of Your Environment

My mom told me as a kid, "You are the people you hang around with." While I resisted her wisdom at that time, I know now it is true. Today I would take that great statement even further and say, "You are a product of all that you surround yourself with!" That includes the tv you watch, the newspapers you read, the friends you have, the movies you watch, your hobbies, your interest, your family, and everything else that are involved with.

Every winter season the news people spend hours each day convincing you and your family that the flu season is coming and that you're susceptible and that millions of people will get the flu. They used to call them epidemics and now they call them pandemics. Do I think that people actually get the flu because it's promoted with such dedication? Absolutely! The media gets everyone thinking about the flu, worrying about the flu, talking about the flu and people will start to think they're getting flu until finally they do get it!

When the media starts promoting recessions

and tough times people everywhere tighten up and this perpetuates that which was promoted. Entire economies can be frozen by what is promoted on television and newspapers! Entire nations of people's attitudes can be shifted from positive to negative in order to influence the actions of many so just a few benefit! The newspapers and televisions have been used for years to influence the attitudes and actions of the many. If millions of people's actions can be altered by the news, certainly your attitude can influence one other person for the good or the bad.

Even the "medical profession" agrees that most mental and physical diseases are actually psychosomatic (of the mind). This has been proven with the placebo pills that in many cases result in as much healing as those who took the real medicine. Even though the placebos are nothing but sugar, people believe it will help them and it so it does!

I believe that the single most valuable asset I have in my life is my ability to stay positive when everyone else is losing their minds. When everyone around me is freaking out and worrying and crying the blues, I choose to stay positive. By staying positive you become the obvious leader, and people will follow your lead. If that position in life is desirable to you, then you need to do everything possible to protect your attitude from things that bring you down. You'll also need to take a preventative step and guard yourself against other people who may have the agenda of affecting you negatively.

It is not enough to just be positive, you have to actually protect yourself against those who are being negative! Watch out for friends, family, work associates and others around you that have the agenda of negatively impacting those around them. Attitudes, like diseases, are contagious. Your enemies are not your problem when it comes to attitude, it's the people closest to you. Would you let your best friend leave his garbage in your house? Of course not! But that's exactly what he's doing when he comes over and starts telling you bad news, gossip and all his troubles. You're allowing his mental trash to be left in your environment and you become infected.

Tips to Have a Great Attitude

If you aren't getting paid the way you want to and you know what you're doing, I assure you that your attitude is part of your problem! If you want a bigger paycheck, get a bigger attitude. The question is, how to you change it, how do you stay positive, what can you do to ensure that you're smiling, happy and loving life?

Here are some helpful suggestions that I've

used in my life when I wanted to make sure I had a beaming, positive attitude.

1) Avoid newspapers, television and radio.

2) Stay away from "can't do" people, people that have trouble in life and people that don't do well. You can try to help people but don't hang around with them and be affected negatively. This includes family and friends.

3) Get everyone in your life on the same page with where you are going and what you want in your life and what is expected of them in order for you to get there!

4) Avoid drugs and alcohol because of the negative influence they have on your mind. They make you lethargic, slow and not sure! Prescription drugs affect the mind as badly as the street drugs and some are proving even more dangerous. Just look at the side effects and warning labels. Control your attitude by being aware and alert, not by being drugged and numbed.

5) Avoid hospitals and doctors if at all possible. Go see them when you absolutely have to but that's it. I've seen too many people get worse after they spend time with doctors and hospitals. Hospitals appear to be "sick factories" rather than places that heal people. Just watch people as they leave.

6) Treat negative talk like garbage. Put up a

sign in your home and your office that reads, NO NEGATIVE TALK ZONE. Don't allow people to talk negatively around you. You don't need it. Treat it like garbage and don't allow anyone to leave their garbage in your environment.

7) Start the Negativity Diet today. Commit to no negative thoughts, ideas or talk for the next twenty-four hours. This will be a start to your really getting control of your thoughts and actions and will help you build discipline to control how you think and act. Thoughts come before actions and your actions then determine your life. Once you get control of how you think, you will then get control of your actions. The negativity diet works likes this: No negative thoughts, talk or actions for a full twenty-four hours or your restart the clock. While this may seem like a very simple challenge I have never met anyone that made it the first twenty-four hours and know thousands of people that failed the challenge only ten minutes after starting.

This is going to give you a game to play whereby you are competing with yourself to start controlling how you think, act and live life! People have become unaware of just how negative they are and then wonder why they get negative results in life! Control your thoughts and you will control your actions. This simple game will first make you aware! Once aware, a person can start making changes. Be gently honest with yourself while playing this game. When you fail, become aware of the negative thought or action, write it down, and restart the clock. Keep doing this until you are able to make it twenty-four hours. Then see how many days you can go. The goal is to create awareness and discipline in what you choose to think and do in your life!

If you want to know how to permanently get rid of negativity call my office and they will introduce you to the only guaranteed surefire way to rid yourself of all your negative computations, ideas, and reactive responses whereby you will be the positive, forward-looking, solution oriented person that you are supposed to be. The reality is if you didn't have any negativity going on in the fist place you wouldn't need the negativity diet. Call 800-368-5771 and my office will turn you on to the most exciting adventure of your life.

Nothing in your life will pay you more rewards than your ability to have and maintain a great attitude. Nothing will prove more valuable in life than a positive outlook on life. People will remember you in life not for how much money you made or your success, but for how you handled life and how you made others feel. Your attitude and your ability to have a positive influence on the attitudes of others will not only affect your sales, but every area of your life: your marriage, your kids, your health, your wealth, your luck- *everything*. You name it and a great attitude will affect it!

Chapter Sixteen Questions:

The author states that people will pay for what

1)

2)

3)

What two things will make you unstoppable:

1)

2)

What are some ways you can treat people like millionaires?

1)

2)

3)

What does the author suggest is your single most valuable asset?

What are some tips for improving your attitude?

1)

2)

3)

4)

Any questions? Call 800-368-5771

THE BIGGEST SALE
OF
MY LIFE

The first moment I saw Elena, I knew I'd found the girl I was going to marry. I was absolutely and completely sold from the first moment I saw her. It also became almost immediately apparent that like many customers I have had, she wasn't going to make this sale very easy for me. I was taken back by her beauty even to the point of being insecure at my qualifications to have her and my ability to get her attention. I pushed through my fears and introduced myself to her as my heart skipped and my pulse raced. She responded to me with complete disinterest as though she couldn't even see me. You would have thought I was a ghost that was unable to be seen. I was devastated and certain by her response that this sale would be almost impossible. The whole encounter lasted maybe a minute when she continued on with what she was doing and left me to be by myself.

I went to one of the people on the set, a friend (working my powerbase) and found out everything he knew about her and got him to give me her phone number. He was reluctant to do so but could see I was never going to leave without getting a way to contact her (hard sell). I called her the following day with enthusiasm and my great attitude convincing myself that I could get her interested in me (attitude is senior to product). Again it didn't go the way I was hoping and she still seemed completely uninterested in my product (me) and was a bit annoyed that I'd called her. I knew I was missing the mark, but was totally convinced that she was the one (completely sold on the product).

I was unable to really get in communication with her because I didn't know what really liked or had an interest in. I was getting nowhere fast, but I refused to give up. Looking for some positive support and reassurances I called my mom and announced that I'd met the girl I was going to marry. My mom was excited and asked if we'd been out yet. I told her that there was just one little problem in that the girl had no interest in me. My mom, wanting to protect her son from being hurt offered her advice on this situation stating, "Grant, it takes two for a relationship. If she isn't interested in you then you can't impose yourself on her." (Protect yourself from negative information - Be careful where you get advice from when you are going after your dreams and goals as even the people that love you the most can offer information that could possibly cause you to get off the path of your dreams.)

The moment my mother said, "It takes two," it hit me what I had to do. If the sale is meant to be, it's up to me! I've heard salespeople blame the customer for years for sales they didn't make. I immediately became even more determined to make this relationship happen.

If someone is to be sold it's up to me, not to Elena. If I wait for her to make it happen it never will, so I had to get creative. Buyers don't buy until someone sells! And it doesn't take two, it only takes one. I decided at that moment that I'd be the one to take complete responsibility for selling myself to her and closing the deal. What to do first: get sold on the product again (me). So I sat down and wrote all the things that I had to offer and all the quality points that I'd bring to the relationship. I then came up with an action plan. I started calling anyone that might know her and put it out there that I was interested in her and wanted to make it known (massive action). Then I decided to call her monthly until I was able to finally break through to her and really get into communication, with her giving me the chance to get to know her and her to get to know me. I called her monthly for an entire year leaving nice little positive messages. Not only did she not take any of my calls but she never returned even a single one of them. But that didn't stop me as no real salesperson will stop because of a little rejection. I just stayed interested and kept letting my interest be known. I was unreasonable and disregarded any logic. As the phone calls were not getting traction, I continued, when necessary, to remind myself that my product was good and my mission was great!

I went back to working my powerbase. I discovered, through persistence, that a friend of mine had a friend that was actually a girlfriend of Elena. I then started by getting to know the girlfriend and I told her that I was interested in Elena and updated her on my efforts and lack of success (powerbase). I asked her to put in a good word for me and to find out what the deal with Elena was and why she wasn't responding to me. The girlfriend actually told me that Elena had mentioned my name before, saying there was this guy who kept calling and leaving funny messages, but that she didn't have any interest.

The girlfriend said that she told Elena I was a really good guy and that she should go out with me. As the girlfriend told me, I got so excited thinking, *I'm going to pull this off*, at which point the girlfriend tried to let me down gently saying that Elena had stated that I just wasn't her type.

Is that a complaint or an objection? I wondered. What is the objection? I had to pull it out of the girlfriend because I had to know what I was dealing with. I got Elena's girlfriend to tell me because I had to know (be committed). She finally told me that Elena had said that I was too short, that she didn't like businessmen and that I just wasn't her type.

But those aren't real reasons not to go out with me, they are just complaints, I thought. (know the difference between complaints and objections).

While all common sense was telling me to give up, I was walking down the street and saw this ugly guy with this beautiful girl and I thought, *how did he do that?* I didn't know the answer, but I knew it wasn't because he quit. So I decided I wouldn't quit until I at least got an appointment, sold the product (me) and at least went for the close!

I had to agree with her first as that is the number one rule in selling. So I called her and left another message on her recorder, probably my thirteenth by now. "Hey, Elena this is Grant. As you probably know, I've been bugging Erica about you. Look, I don't want you to think I am a stalker or anything, just a guy that's really interested in you and I have no intention of giving up until you give me a chance. By the way, just as an update – I'm growing." I always kept the messages positive and upbeat and never made her feel wrong.

One day I was asking a buddy of mine about Elena, whom he'd also been trying to date. He told me she wasn't really interested in a relationship, but was more into shooting guns and her career as an actress. He was actually giving me reasons why she wasn't much of a catch (sounds like a salesman that couldn't close a deal). I then pursued this information regarding shooting and found out that Elena was one of the top ten women clay shooters in the state of California and that shooting was her passion. I called the L.A. Gun Club, rented the shooting range and hired the best coach in Los Angeles for the following Saturday. I then called her again leaving another message on her recorder telling her that I had booked the club and the trainers and was asking her out for a day of shooting. (Find out what they are interested in not what you are interested in). Sixty seconds later she called me back for the first time! We had our first real encounter that Saturday and we were married less than a year later.

My wife was the toughest sale I'd ever made and I can tell you it was worth it. I have been in deals as large as $80 million but it didn't even compare to getting this girl to first pay attention to me, then go out with me and later to be able to propose to her and know she would say yes.

My wife will tell you today that I saw us long before she did and that my conviction and complete knowingness of us as a couple was very difficult to resist. She will not say that I imposed or pressured or stalked her. She'll tell you that I predicted the future and created it by knowing what I wanted, staying with it and continuing to do whatever was necessary to get the deal done. My wife would not say that I sold her in some negative context but rather that I showed my love for her and put it all out there, regardless of her response to me (Give-Give-Give).

I will tell you that the most important sale of my life was this sale and also that if it were not for my view of selling as a needed skill in life and an understanding of it technically, I would not have been able to get this worthy close.

Summary

Your ability to persuade others determines by itself how well you will do in all areas of your life. Selling is an absolute necessity for really living life and making your dreams come true. While selling is a career for many, it's a requirement for all. You need to sell, negotiate and persuade others in life to get what you want. How well you can do that will determine what kind of life you will have and how many people you can influence.

Become a student of this thing called selling. Don't treat it like some distasteful thing you have to do or that you'll hire others to do. Selling is the ultimate fuel of every economy on planet earth and without people selling ideas and concepts and products, the world would never improve. If you want to make a difference on this planet, learn how to sell. If you want to make sure your worthy ideas get known to the world, you'll have to sell. If you want your way in life, if you want your company to do well, if you want your family to prosper, learn the information in this book, and I guarantee that you will prosper in ways others considered impossible.

Thank you and remember to keep Selling — your life depends on it!

Grant Cardone

Chapter Seventeen Questions:

Write an essay of what you learned from this chapter and from this book and how you are going to apply that in order to get what you want in life:

ABOUT THE AUTHOR

Grant Cardone has been speaking to audiences around the world for over twenty years on sales, success, finance, real estate and motivation. His dynamic energy, humorous and fast paced delivery keeps audiences entertained, intrigued and involved.

Mr. Cardone is the CEO of two training and consulting companies and owns a real estate investment and development firm worth over $100,000,000 in real estate holdings.

Mr. Cardone has been interviewed on the Fox's Money for Breakfast, the Today Show, Access Hollywood and MSNBC as well as a guest on over

250 radio shows. He is presently working on two more books, *The Closers' Almanac* and *Breaking Out From the Middle Class.*

He lives in Los Angeles with his wife, actress and producer, Elena Lyons.

GRANT CARDONE
BEST SELLING AUTHOR

Rules of Success
These rules weren't made to be broken.

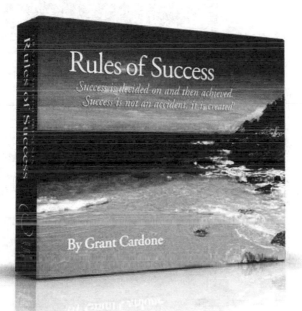

Grant Cardone's audio program, **The Rules of Success** is the ultimate guide to fuel your attitude into non-stop, positive action. With 13 strategy-packed discs, these rules will guarantee you the attitude, approach, and confidence to grab hold of that success and make you realize that these rules *weren't* made to be broken.

Don't WAIT for success, CREATE it.

call **800-368-5771**   or visit   **GrantCardone.com**

GRANT GC CARDONE
BEST SELLING AUTHOR

Hearing is
believing...

You've read the book, now hear it read straight from the author himself! With the **Sell to Survive Audio Program**, you not only get a full reading of the book from Grant but priceless additional commentary giving a full understanding to the strategies. These are 7 discs that will forever change your selling career!

Order this program now and learn how to get anything you want in life!

126 Closes. 8 Discs.
Unlimited $uccess.

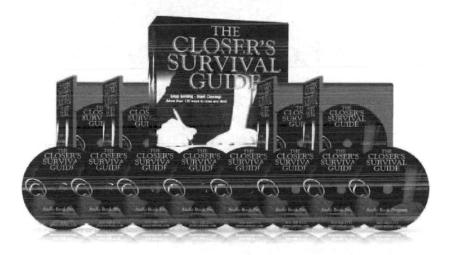

The Close is 20% of your selling time but 100% of your income. **The Closers' Survival Guide Audio Series** contains 8 discs of closes that will make you a Master of Closing. Grant personally delivers 126 of the sickest, most powerful closes known to man while giving you the secrets to full utilization of each close so that you can shut the deal down.

Become a Master of Closing with Grant's Closer's Survival Guide!

call **800-368-5771**   or visit **GrantCardone.com**

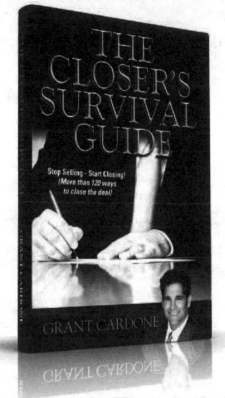

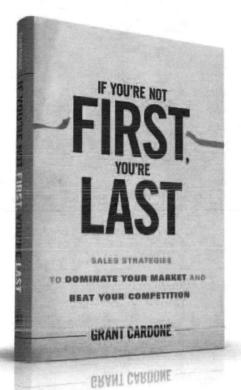

STOP THE NEGATIVITY!

Get Grant Cardone's
"No Negativity" poster for your:

- Office
- Home
- Company
- As a gift

It's all about staying positive and saying NO to negativity!

call 800-368-5771 or visit **GrantCardone.com**

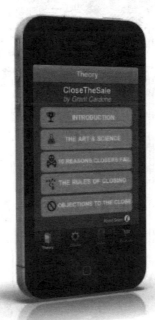

Cardone University
Become a Master.

Do you want to _____ **?**

    a.) Reach your potential
    b.) Earn more money
    c.) Achieve success
    d.) All of the above

Then **Cardone University** is exactly what you need. This is Grant's new on-demand sales training university available 24 hours a day, 7 days a week. In short, concise segments, Grant delivers unstoppable strategies that will guarantee that nothing gets in the way of your professional success.

For more information and to access a free trial, visit:

CardoneUniversity.com